Daily Inspiration
From Scriptural Symbols

Philip M. Hudson

Copyright 2017 by Philip M. Hudson.
The book author retains sole copyright to his contributions to this book.

Published 2017.
Printed in the United States of America.

All rights reserved.

No portion of this book may be reproduced, stored in a retrieval system, or transmitted in any form or by any means – electronic, mechanical, photocopy, recording, scanning, or other – except for brief quotations in critical reviews or articles, without the prior written permission of the author.

ISBN 978-1-943650-43-9

Library of Congress Control Number 2017931673

Illustrations - Google Images.

This book was published by BookCrafters
Parker, Colorado.
www.bookcrafters.net

This book may be ordered from
online bookstores.

Table of Contents

Acknowledgements..1
Preface..3
Introduction..5
Calendar...13
Author's Note...395
Appendix (List of Scripture Citations)..399
About the Author...411
Also by The Author..413

Acknowledgements

I have attributed quotations to original authors whenever possible, as well as when I have editorialized their thoughts. In many cases, however, my language will naturally reflect the teachings of leaders and members of The Church of Jesus Christ of Latter-day Saints.

The list of those who have contributed their ideas to the construction of this calendar is endless. As I have collected my own thoughts, I have realized how heavily I have borrowed from the towering examples of those who, over the years, have been my mystical mentors, my sensible chaperones, my spiritual guides, my surrogate saviors, my compassionate critics, and everything in between.

They are my avatars, the manifestations of deity in bodily forms, my na'vi, the visionaries who communicate with God on a level to which I can only aspire, and my tsaddik, whom I esteem as the interpreters of biblical law and scripture. They are my divine teachers incarnate.

They have shown me the way, stretched my mind, reinforced my faith, strengthened my testimony, lifted my spirits, helped me to discover my wings, provided of their means, given immaterial support, emboldened me with words of encouragement, cheered me on with wise counsel, taught me humility, been there to steady me, soothed my troubled soul, stepped in to nurture me, led me to fountains of living water, wet my parched lips with inspired counsel, bound up my wounds, offered listening ears, and extended open arms.

Every teacher, student, classmate, business associate, friend, mentor, family member, priesthood and relief society brother, sister, or leader, ordinance worker, and temple patron with whom I have come in contact has influenced me. Every author, poet, journalist, essayist, thespian, satirist, and lyricist with whom I have become familiar has moved me in some positive way. I have tried to find the silk purse in every sow's ear, and the silver lining in every cloud. If I have been given a lemon, I have done my best to follow the recipe for lemonade. I have learned not to cry because it's over, but to smile because I was privileged to have had the experience. I have discovered how to see the opportunity in every difficulty, and I have found that when I keep my face to the sun, the shadows are always behind me.

I have come to know that there is so much good in the worst of us, and so much bad in the best of us, that it hardly behooves any of us to talk about the rest of us. I try to keep tempests in their teapots where they belong, and to keep adversity in perspective. I have witnessed change, that so often comes like a flash of lightning and a clap of thunder. I have seen the people shrink in fear, but I know that after the storm, flowers will bloom. ("I Ching"). I try to retain the joyful anticipation of the optimistic little boy, who, when faced with the daunting task of shoveling up an enormous pile of manure in a horse stall near his home, enthusiastically set about his task with the exclamation: "There's got to be a pony in there, somewhere!"

Well did the poet teach: "No man is an island, entire of itself. Every man is a piece of the continent; a part of the main. If a clod be washed away by the sea, Europe is the less, as well as if a promontory were, as well as if a manor of thy friends or of thine own were. Any man's death diminishes me, because I am involved in mankind. Therefore, never send to know for whom the bell tolls. It tolls for thee." (John Donne).

Even now, when I think of the multitude of angels thinly disguised as my family, friends, and peers who have ministered to my needs, I remember the words of Sir Isaac Newton, who, when pressed to reveal the great secret behind his accomplishments, simply replied: "I stood on the shoulders of giants." Of course, at the end of the day, with the obvious exception of the scripture I have chosen as the illustration for each date's entry, I alone am responsible for the content of this volume. I hope my interpretation of principles will cultivate your interest to dig deeper into the themes woven into the tapestry of the scriptures, by studying first-hand their related doctrines, and by simultaneously seeking inspiration from the Spirit. My only goal is to help you to expand your insights into the foundation truths and celestial guideposts that I have attempted to embed within this calendar of thoughts that have been inspired by my love of the scriptures.

Preface

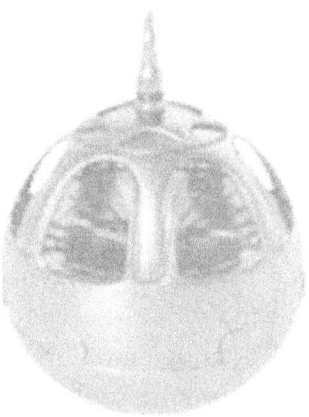

In The Book of Mormon, Nephi expressed his reluctance to teach his people concerning "the manner of the Jews," at the same time revealing: "My soul delighteth in the words of Isaiah, for I came out from Jerusalem, and mine eyes hath beheld the things of the Jews, and I know that the Jews do understand the things of the prophets, and there is none other people that understand the things which were spoken unto the Jews like unto them, save it be that they are taught after the manner of the things of the Jews." (2 Nephi 25:6, see Alma 11:4). His encouragement to study The Book of Mormon against the backdrop of Nephite culture underscores the price we must pay in order to understand the manner of prophesying among the Jews.

Because the prophets in Israel employed types and shadows, metaphors and similes, and idioms and symbols, and because their messages were often dualistic, if we first understand the historical context in which they were written, and then ponder words, verses, chapters, and books, we are better able to read between the lines and discern multiple layers of meaning.

Although that may be a stratospheric standard of inquiry that is far beyond the scope of this book, it does set the stage for independent gospel study by orienting our sight on the stars, no matter where on the vast ocean of life we might find ourselves. At first, getting a fix on the symbolism that comes alive with intentional imagery and magical metaphor might seem like a daunting task. But soon, these messages from the scriptures will transcend time and loom larger than life.

The Lord declared: "Now behold, a marvelous work is about to come forth among the children of men." (D&C 4:1). The key to comprehension by our inquisitive minds of that spectacular meteor shower of stunning scripture is to learn to embrace truth wherever it may be found. Then, we shall "know mysteries which are great and marvelous." (D&C 6:11). A cascading cornucopia of comprehension awaits us when we have learned how to tap directly into the power of God. We begin to experience the wonder of the promise that "by the power of the Holy Ghost (we) may know the truth of all things." (Moroni 10:5). Thus, did the Lord admonish the Nephites: "Now behold, I say unto you, that ye ought to search these things. Yea, a commandment I give unto you that ye search these things diligently." (3 Nephi 23:1).

When we have done as the Savior has commanded, the scriptures will flow easily and poetically to our minds. Persistence will lead to practiced fluency that is the inevitable result of memorization, recitation, individual and cooperative study, comparison with companion scriptures, expansion of understanding by critical analysis of supportive commentaries, and inspiration that follows faith, fasting, and prayer. It is my hope that this book will enlighten your own process of inquiry, as you are cast off into a stream of revelation and carried along in the quickening currents of experience with the Spirit.

Introduction

The scriptures accompanying the thoughts in this volume reflect the symbolism that has always been a prominent feature of prophetic writing. A symbol is simply one thing that is the representation of something else. Because language itself is symbolic, when you crack open this book, you will begin by reading letters that make up words that are linked together into sentences that phonetically depict concepts with which you are familiar. During the process, your mind will automatically collate around 43,000 word symbols that range from the simple to the profoundly complex.

For example, the word G-O-D is prominently illustrated, occurring over 257 times. The symbolism behind the concept these three letters represent has changed the world. The ancient Hebrews, who dared not utter His sacred name, used the symbol Y-H-W-H (Yahweh or "Jehovah") instead, literally meaning: "I Am Who I Am." Such symbolism traces a trajectory that leaves fairy dust in its wake. It transcends depth, breadth, and height. Its scope not only defies space, but even time, because it illuminates the far reaches of eternity. Perhaps this is why God has symbolically defined Himself as Alpha and Omega, the First and the Last, the Beginning and the End, and without beginning of days or end of years. It is remarkable that it is within the capacity of our mortal minds to grasp, at least superficially, these symbols that are profoundly associated with the eternal world.

Symbols lubricate the melodic flow of the recitation of scripture. We can almost palpably feel our minds wrap around the symbolism of entire chapters of text. This leads to our grasp of the collective symbolism of the Bible itself. Symbolism helps to soothe our spirits, and it creates order in a chaotic world. It facilitates our faith in systematic organizations of religious dogma; for example, that which is neatly compartmentalized as Catholicism, or Evangelism, or even Mormonism. It allows us to embrace entire religious movements, for example, the Reformation and the Restoration. On a grand scale, we maintain purposeful focus by using symbols to answer the questions encompassed within the Plan of Salvation, relating to where we came from, why we are here, and where we are going. We define our divine purpose with symbols and drape it with a coat of many colors that is the centerpiece of the collective wardrobe known as the Plan of Salvation, that is itself anchored to the Atonement of Jesus Christ. This takes us back to the being of God. We simply call Him "Father," which flows easily from our lips and is perhaps the greatest symbol of all.

Overlapping brain-maps enhance and potentiate our five somatic senses of sight, smell, taste, touch, and hearing. We become totally immersed in our experiences, enveloped by inner stirrings that simply cannot be rationally explained by the neurochemical activation of living tissue, or even by the firestorm of hormonal secretions. We feel tingling sensations that cannot be explained by optic and auditory nerve stimulation alone. We feel a burning in our bosom, and describe it as a tangible immersion in the element of spirit. At these moments, symbolism becomes the unconscious catalyst potentiating the emotions that permeate life's trials and tribulations, as well as its golden moments. We begin to see what God meant, when He told Joseph Smith: "All these things shall give thee experience." (D&C 122:7). But we also see why Lehi declared: "Men are that they might have joy." (2 Nephi 2:25).

The ability of oral and written symbols to shape our minds is staggering. We have an incredibly powerful capacity to incorporate symbols into our collective consciousness. According to the Global Language Monitor (languagemonitor.com) there are 6,912 languages and dialects on earth. The various Chinese vernaculars alone utilize about 50,000 ideograms. In his complete works, Shakespeare employed something on the order of 29,000 different words, about 1,700 of which were his own invention. There are about 20,000 different words in the King James Translation of the Bible, and a mind-boggling total of 995,112 words (give or take a few) in the English language. William Tyndale, the author of the first translation of the New Testament to be printed in English, (1526), coined the words "Jehovah," and "Atonement," that have become powerfully symbolic words in our familiar latter-day scriptures.

Most of do reasonably well navigating through life by utilizing only a fraction of the word symbols that are available to us. We communicate with others and personally interpret the world around us through sensory input and perceptual processing, and we remain on solid ground as long as we stick with our native tongue and don't stray off course into any of the other 6,911 languages and dialects. Albert Einstein's wife was once asked if she understood her husband's explanation of his theories of relativity. She said she understood the words, but not the sentences. That brings to mind another symbol, one that more than any other perhaps, has helped to shape our future: $E = MC^2$. With the possible exception of G.O.D., there probably exists on earth no other symbol that is so simple to articulate and yet is so mentally, emotionally, and spiritually complex; that is so universally recognized, and yet is so little understood.

The brilliant theoretical physicist, Steven Hawking, wrote a watered-down version of his trail-blazing work on space-time, entitled "A Brief History of Time." It attained a cult following, and graced millions of coffee tables around the world. That it was seldom actually read, and difficult to understand when it was, doesn't change the fact that it quickly became a symbol of our desire to recognize, acknowledge, and conceptually wrestle with some of the most challenging physical concepts that have flowed from the minds, pens, and computer keyboards of our academic icons.

But God has trumped even Einstein and Hawking; He has created a personal learning laboratory in the hallowed halls of grey matter within our cerebral hemispheres, that we might come to grips with not only the mathematical equations of the physical universe, but also the metaphysical permutations of philosophical and religious thought. He has given each of us more than enough neural pathways to deal with the great issues of life, and more particularly to ponder the solemnities of eternity. Within our brains, each of our one hundred billion neurons has a direct connection via dendrites to sixty other neural axons. The possible combinations are virtually endless; something on the order of six thousand billion, which dwarfs the capacity of the Internet.

In fact, researchers have discovered that, unlike a classical computer that codes information as ones and zeroes in a linear pathway, a brain cell simultaneously uses over two-dozen different avenues to code its bits of information. They have calculated that the brain has a storage capacity of at least 1 petabyte, or a billion billion bytes, of data. What's more, the human brain can utilize this mind-boggling amount of information with the expenditure of only 20 watts of power, which is equivalent to that needed to run a child's night light. A digital computer with the same memory and processing power would require 1 gigawatt, roughly the power output of an entire nuclear power generating station.

But I digress. To sharpen the point, as I slowly work my way back to the thesis of this introduction, consider this: A one hundred forty pound human being is made up of roughly ten trillion cells, and each one is composed of twenty billion protein molecules. Each protein molecule has, on average, fourteen thousand atoms. Each of those has around forty-nine matter particles, consisting of a nucleus, protons, and electrons, etc.. Each of those average matter particles is composed of roughly one million photons, which are the basic units of electro-magnetic energy. Thus, the human body is one-billionth particle matter, composed of substance, and the rest is photons. Joseph Smith, as it turns out, was right on the mark. He trumped the best and brightest minds of the twenty-first century, when he wrote: "That which is of God is light; and he that receiveth light, and continueth in God, receiveth more light; and that light groweth brighter and brighter until the perfect day." (D&C 50:24). In 1831, 48 years before Einstein was born, Joseph Smith already knew by his own experience that, fundamentally, we are beings of light, and he used beautiful poetic symbolism to clothe his point. (See Joseph Smith History 1:17 & 30).

He had been taught that we communicate on more than a somatic level, and that the energy that drives us cannot be easily quantified or described, for we radiate with light. "Have ye spiritually been born of God?" asked Alma. "Have ye received his image in your countenances? Have ye experienced this mighty change in your hearts?" (Alma 5:14). Those who have drawn upon this universal energy, and have recognized the source of its power, have relied upon symbolism when no other description would do. They have inadequately called it the Great Ocean of Thought, the Ashia, Ka, Teotl, the Force, Prana, Mana, the Great Spirit, Chakra, Yin/Yang, and Tai Ch'i-Tao, but we know it as the Light of Christ.

We enter mortality leaving the stardust of symbolism scattered in our wake, as "children coming down like gentle rain through darkened skies, with glory trailing from their feet as they go, and endless promise in their eyes." (Doug Stewart). Truly, did the poet observe: "Our birth is but a sleep and a forgetting. The soul that rises with us, our life's star, hath had elsewhere its setting, and cometh from afar. Not in entire forgetfulness, and not in utter nakedness, but trailing clouds of glory do we come, from God, Who is our Home." (William Wordsworth).

These poets and others have symbolically described our place in the Cosmos as a dwelling that is at once intensely private, and yet is molded by our communal interaction. But ultimately, we feather only those nests that are uniquely our own. No-one is permitted to enter the inner sanctum without our permission. Esau sold his birthright for a mess of pottage, evoking images that reflect far more than the forfeiture of a meal, or of personal possessions. In fact, he profaned a very special relationship and lost his personal identity as a chosen vessel of God, to put it symbolically.

Symbols that are peculiar to a given culture are idioms, whose meaning "cannot be deduced from the literal definitions and the arrangements of their parts, but refers instead to a figurative meaning that is known only through common use." ("Wikipedia"). The operative words here are "common use." Sometimes, with repetition, idioms crash through the firewalls thrown up by cultural bias and boundaries. For example, we enjoy commonality with the ancient Greeks because we study, and apply to our own circumstances, classical literature. However, without the clarification that comes with dedicated scholarship, the achievements of their civilization would be "Greek" to us. Similarly, we understand Isaiah, in spite of the fact that he lived over two and a half millennia ago, because our religious culture promotes scriptural scholarship and values familiarity with the nuance of his unique style. The clarity expressed in symbolism is particularly true of his writings that are inordinately represented in this volume. In general, though, idiomatic speech becomes ours as we study any culture that coined terms or phrases that were once uniquely theirs.

Our understanding of symbolism facilitates our transition to higher spiritual planes. Symbols possess layers of meaning, making recognition as enjoyable as eating an artichoke. Symbols lift us to an expansive comprehension of our spiritual reserves. Our universal familiarity with a variety of symbols facilitates our collective understanding, and makes it simultaneously meaningful on multiple levels to any random group of people who have been exposed to the doctrines of the kingdom. In this sense, God is no respecter of persons.

Symbols touch our chords of commonality, rooting our faith in familiarity, no matter at what point we may be on the path of progression. The Spirit exercises our affinity for symbolism by touching those who preach, teach, expound, and exhort. It encourages them to slip into the use of metaphor and simile to embrace their audiences, to create memorable statements of faith, and to reach conclusions designed to harmonize intellectual and religious inquiry.

Soapboxes are inherently symbolic, and those who stand on bully pulpits to promote social, political, and even ecclesiastical agendas often gain the attention of the curious crowd by tantalizing them with symbolism that has been woven into their rhetoric. Great orators have used symbolism, but even common speech can be peppered with symbols that have the power to get our adrenalin pumping, light up our minds with inspiration, tug at our heartstrings, or open the floodgates of our tear ducts. In every case, the use of a good symbol can help to drive a point home, and when it does, it is invariably well received.

Today, we live in a world where information is dispensed in thirty-second sound bites and where teachers compete for the attention of students who are accustomed to being bombarded with a stroboscopic barrage of images during six hours of television, P.D.A.s, and video games every day. Children are influenced as they have always been by symbols, but parents are beginning to lose control of the connection that has been forged by our familiarity with culturally stable symbolism. Today, that platform of permanency is being seditiously eroded, and more than ever before, we must very carefully guard the symbols that we have always relied upon as our revelatory rock-stars. Only if they are carefully maintained through vigorous exercise and judicious use, and if they are nourished by careful and prayerful scholarship, will they retain the power to cast us off into the aforementioned streams of personal revelation where we may be carried along in the quickening currents of direct experience with God.

Almost by default, the media with their hidden agendas are increasingly entrusted with the transmission to the rising generation of the symbols that have been the centerpieces of our society, and even of our civilization. For this reason alone, religious educators must not abdicate their primary responsibility to use the vivid imagery of symbolism, to help us to retain our familiarity with and love of scriptures and ordinances that are laced with idiomatic speech. For all things have their likeness, and all things are created and made to bear record of God. (See Moses 6:63). Our Latter-day Saint tradition utilizes symbolism that is in "accord one with another – that which is earthly conforming to that which is heavenly." (D&C 128:9). It is for this very reason that the symbolism of the scriptures can be profoundly moving, enlarging our comprehension beyond that which we would have normally expected to enjoy through mortal experience devoid of such dogma. Thus, symbolism forges powerful links between the secular and the divine. This work, then, is offered as a tool to help us to better understand the literary gift of symbolism, that we might deepen our testimonies of the providence of our Father, of the divine mission of our Redeemer, and of the nurturing influence of the Holy Ghost.

January 1

"But
who may
abide the day
of his coming? And
who shall stand when
he appeareth? For he is
like a refiner's fire, and
like fuller's soap."
(Malachi 3:2).

Life is
made up
of an endless
chain of spiritual
experiences that are
balanced by the constant
counterpoint of worldliness.
At first blush, there appears to
be a wide gulf between the spiritual
and the temporal, that one would think
might make things easier for the righteous.
These contrasting sides of our nature seem
to be incompatible. But without a working
knowledge of the principles of the Plan, it
would be much more difficult to reconcile
the two and enjoy a state of holiness as
our natural habitat, richer for having
had our mortal experiences. We are
not to be worn down by life, or to
be overcome by evil influences,
but rather to be refined and
purified by adversity, by
danger, by misfortune,
and by challenges.

January 2

"Thus
shall ye eat (of
the Passover meal)
with your loins girded,
your shoes on your feet,
and your staff in your
hand, and ye shall
eat it in haste."
(Exodus 12:11).

As we jog
along at a measured
pace upon the pathway
of progress, and we negotiate
the twists and turns of mortality
while enjoying the aerobic exercise of
free will, it always helps to have celestial
sign posts to guide us through the telestial
traffic jams and conceptual cul-de-sacs that
threaten to detour us from the straight and
narrow way. The expanding circles of our
opportunity, afforded by our obedience
to gospel principles, assures each us of
that we will have direct exposure to
the perfect law of liberty. Thereby,
we abandon the tortuous route
through Idumea that is taken
by those bound for telestial
glory. Instead, we follow
the unmistakable track
that inevitably leads
to celestial surety
in a heavenly
setting.

January 3

Those who have
hardened their hearts are
able to understand less and less
"of the word, until they know nothing
concerning the mysteries of the kingdom"
of God, until they "are taken captive by the
devil." When they have reached that point,
their actions are no longer determined by
their exercise of free will, but rather "by
his will, down to destruction. Now
this is what is meant by the
chains of hell."
(Alma 12:11).

The prince of the power of
the air, who is a roaring lion, the angel
of the bottomless pit, and a ruler of darkness, is
always prodding and probing our defenses for signs of
weakness in the fortress that is our spiritual security. His
temptations of pleasure and advantage are adroit and they
are insidious. And then, when we have capitulated to his
influences and engage in the habit pattern of sin, we feel
increasingly uncomfortable in the company of the more
righteous members of our communities. At the same
time, as we spiral inevitably downward into the
abyss of apostasy, our free will and power to
change slip away. The gates of hell loom
large, while the weight of the chains
of Satan becomes oppressive for
us to bear, because we become
thoroughly entrenched in
behaviors that are self
defeating.

January 4

"The Lord
shall make the
rain of thy hand
powder and dust.
From heaven shall it
come down upon thee,
until thou be destroyed."
(Deuteronomy 28:24).

Our
great and terrible
judgment comes not
at some hazy point in the
future, but today. We speak,
think, and act according to either
celestial, terrestrial, or telestial laws.
Each of us has been blessed with a moral
compass. Our faith in Christ with its evidence
in action, clearly marks the path that we have
chosen to follow. Each day that we live, we are
24 hours closer to the Pleasing Bar of Christ. If
we have committed the 13th Article of Faith to
practice as well as to memory, its principles
will have become the particles of our faith.
"We believe in being honest, true, chaste,
benevolent, and in doing good to all
men. Indeed, we may say that we
follow the admonition of Paul.
If there is anything virtuous,
lovely, or of good report or
praiseworthy, we seek
after these things."
(See Philippians
4:8).

January 5

"He hath made my mouth like a sharp sword. In the shadow of his hand hath he hid me, and made me a polished shaft. In his quiver, hath he hid me."
(Isaiah 49:2).

One of the things that can be most frustrating to members of the church is when their friends and their neighbors do not want to hear the good news. But they need to remind themselves that when the world rejected the Mortal Messiah, He didn't retreat to His home in Galilee. Today, our peers could receive the gospel message differently, but the Lord has given us a proven pattern that we might share His joy. He wants us to know what it is like to feel the Spirit, even to feel as He does; not only the happiness of personally seeing someone come to the knowledge of the truth, but also the pain of rejection, when God's children have refused the invitation to be born again and to taste the fruit of the tree of life.

January 6

"The angels
which kept not their first
estate…he hath reserved in
everlasting chains under darkness
unto the judgment of the great day."
(Jude 1:6).

Each
one of those
who has come
to the earth to fight
the battle raging in the
hearts of men on Saturday
was counted among the most
valiant in the pre-earth existence,
and throughout the propaganda war
that was waged by Satan for control of
the minds of his brothers and sisters, they
were passionate in their defense of free will.
Following that struggle, agency did prevail,
and when the victorious spirits came to the
earth, they did so with a passion for their
hard-won freedom to choose their own
destiny. Therefore, when those spirits
are controlled by compulsion in any
degree of unrighteousness, their
ingrained tendency is to resist.
We need to be very cautious
how we interact with our
youth, when questions
arise that involve the
execution of their
divine right of
free will.

January 7

"For thou
hast been a strength to
the poor (as well as) to the
needy in his distress, a refuge
from the storm, a shadow from
the heat, when the blast of the
terrible ones is as a storm
against the wall."
(Isaiah 25:4).

The Lord has
admonished us to
love our enemies, and
to do good to them, and to
lend, hoping for nothing again;
and our reward shall be great. (See
Luke 6:35). The "get even" mentality
of revenge that has become so popularized
in books and films and reinforced in everyday
interpersonal relationships, in commerce, and social
settings, is antithetical to the gospel of Jesus Christ. It
may be true that in business, you don't get what you
deserve; you get what you negotiate. But when the
earth has been cleansed in order to receive its
paradisiacal glory, a higher standard will
prevail. Before that happens, the Saints
have a responsibility to prepare the
earth for the Millennium, when
the lion and the lamb will
lie down together
in harmony.

January 8

"There was war in
heaven. Michael and
His angels fought against
the dragon, and the dragon lost
and his angels, and prevailed not,
neither was their place found
any more in heaven."
(Revelation 12:7-8).

Zion
and Babylon
are diametrically
opposed, and polarized
in camps at opposite ends
of the spiritual spectrum. They
are, and will forever be, completely
at odds with each other. There is little
common ground upon which substantive
dialogue could ever be introduced, because
the solid foundation pillars upon which Zion
rests are philosophically incompatible with the
detritus scattered about by the forces of Babylon,
that was a repercussion of the War in Heaven. The
theology upon which a Zion society is based allows
its inhabitants to raise their eyes to God for their
redemption, while the apologists and political
pundits of Babylon cannot see beyond the
intellect of man for their salvation, and
can do little more than shrug their
shoulders in resignation when
they hear the clarion call to
amend their behavior
and focus their
faith.

January 9

"Thou
lovest righteousness,
and hatest wickedness.
Therefore…thy God hath
anointed thee with the
oil of gladness."
(Psalms 45:7).

In
response
to the direction
of a benevolent God,
angels have been sent from
heaven to administer the oil of
gladness. It is like having spiritual
angioplasty, facilitating the free flow
of communication between us and God.
It is inspired treatment for sclerosis of the
spirit. Mormon recounted that Ammon, one
of the 4 Sons of Mosiah, had reason to rejoice,
for he had been given a second chance to fulfill
his life's potential, after he had been born again.
He must have considered himself very fortunate
that God had looked beyond the behavior of his
rebellious youth, and had been able to see into
his heart. His rough exterior, as it turned out,
had been nothing more than a façade. His
true character was only revealed when
the Atonement released him from the
awful bondage of sin, and in the
miracle of a spiritual rebirth,
he became a new creature
in the Lord and Savior
Jesus Christ.

January 10

"When
the most High
divided the nations
their inheritance, when he
separated the sons of Adam,
he set the bounds of the people
according to the number of
the children of Israel."
(Deuteronomy 32:8).

If
we deny
the power of
God to influence
our lives, we esteem
as a thing of naught the
suffering endured by His Son,
reject His sacrifice, and refuse His
amazing grace, closing our minds to
the soul expanding opportunities that
are provided for us. We disregard the
invitation to follow Him, and are deaf
to His entreaties. Living only for the
moment, we die to the things of the
Spirit. When we turn our backs to
the light of the gospel, we often
think that we have it all, even
though what we really have
is a shadow, nothing more
than an illusion, and
only a caricature
of reality.

January 11

"The
more part
of all the tribes
have been led away,
and they are scattered to
and fro upon the isles of the
sea, and whither they are
none of us knoweth."
(1 Nephi 22:9).

The familiar
phrase "isles of the
sea" that is found in the
scriptures is an antiquated
Semitic idiom that reflected
the practice of sailing to far-away
places. The continents of Africa and
Asia, by contrast, were characterized as
"the earth" because they were accessible by
land. Idioms are expressions that are peculiar
to a given culture, and we would expect Semitic
examples throughout The Book of Mormon. The
facility with which they have been sprinkled into
its narrative suggests that they were devices that
were frequently employed by legitimate Israelite
authors. It begs credulity to suggest that Joseph
Smith was so adroit that, on his own initiative,
he would have known how to utilize these
colloquialisms throughout the record,
let alone how to situate each one in
an undeniably perfect literary
and cultural context.

January 12

"You
receive no
witness until
after the trial of
your faith."
(Ether 12:6).

Untested potential is
antithetical to the principles of the
Plan. The Lord said: "I will try the faith
of my people." (3 Nephi 26:11). The Book of
Mormon has been given to the world as part of that
self-administered examination. The Saints are compelled
to read it in order to nurture independent testimonies of its
divine authenticity. If they do not wholeheartedly embrace the
doctrine of Christ contained therein, and if they fail to live up to
their covenants, they will be in the power of Satan. The inquisition
that accompanied the grand experiment posited by Alma to the
poor Zoramites portends an ominous consequence. (See Alma
32). None of us will receive a witness until after the trial of
our faith. Only after having passed through the refiner's
fire will we be as tempered steel in our devotion to the
Savior. "I have refined thee," said the Lord, "but not
with silver; I have chosen thee in the furnace of
affliction." (Isaiah 48:10). Tom Paine wrote:
"What we obtain too cheap, we esteem
too lightly. 'Tis dearness alone that
gives everything its value.
Heaven knows how to
put a proper price
on its goods."

January 13

"Lift up thy voice
like a trumpet."
(Isaiah 58:1).

We
share the
Good News in
a hierarchy that is
based on understanding
at first, next on acceptance,
then on commitment, and finally
on recommitment. Preaching is akin
to understanding, teaching to acceptance,
expounding to commitment, and exhortation
to re-commitment. Testimony is an expression of
action that follows the internalization of principles.
It is borne with strenuous effort that reflects the price
that has been paid to understand the voice of the Lord
concerning those principles. Testimony is a reflection of
the value we place on direct experience with the Spirit
as it teaches us about those principles. Testimony is
not free, but is purchased at considerable expense.
Testimony releases the power of principles, their
merit and validity, and empowers us to bind
ourselves to those principles by covenants
of action that increase our strength and
endurance, day by day, as we learn
to rely upon the Lord in all that
we say and everything that
we do. He completes us.
He is both the Author
and the Finisher
of our faith.

January 14

"Then cometh a death" that is "even a second death, which is a spiritual death."
(Alma 12:16).

The idols of our day take on ephemeral identities. It may be a sex symbol, the almighty dollar, a movie queen, eternal youth, governmental paternalism, the ivory towers of academia, or the robes of the false priesthood. It is all the same. Many years ago, one of our most popular magazine was "Life." "People" followed shortly, then "Us." We ended with "Self." Where do we go from there? We suffer spiritual death because of our single-minded self-reliance. It may be the new religion, but it is nothing more than steak without the sizzle. If we are no longer oriented toward eternal principles as our celestial beacon, where will we go for solace, when the next crisis cries out, and we hear our own names being called?

January 15

"If
the
root
be holy,
so are the
branches."
(Romans 11:16).

Zenos
foresaw
that Israel,
represented by
the leafy branches
of the olive tree that
had grown wild, was
grafted in to the natural
tree, in a spiritual rebirth.
The roots and the branches
were equal in strength as they
were nourished by the word of
God. They would embrace each
line upon line and precept upon
precept. Covenant Israel, or the
Gentiles, would grow up beside
Blood Israel, with testimonies of
the Lord. In the millennial day,
it will no longer be as it had
been, when the branches
had grown at a faster
rate than the roots
could bear.

January 16

"The Lord went before them by day in a pillar of a cloud, to lead them the way, and by night in a pillar of fire, to give them light, to go by day and night." (Exodus 13:21).

As we reflect upon the ramifications of our lineage and birthright, we may want to consider the covenant consciousness of the members of The Church of Jesus Christ in the latter days. Sometimes, we forget that Latter-day Saints are also of the House of Israel, either literally or by adoption, and that they too may claim the covenant blessings promised by God so long ago, not only to Abraham, but also to all of his seed.

January 17

"And he commandeth you that ye suffer no ravenous wolf to enter among you."
(Alma 5:60).

We are all influenced by Satan's bribes. He attracts followers with the offer of pleasure or advantage, and as a seducer and a tempter he allures insidiously and adroitly. But it is precisely because the Plan requires opposition that the earth becomes an astonishing learning laboratory, a majestic clockwork, and a perfect 'machine for the making of Gods.' (Henri Bergson). But without the principles, the ordinances, and the covenants of the gospel that hold evil in check, mortality would have become nothing more than a malicious trap or a snare of Satan; and if he were to be given free-reign to attack the fold, his ravenous wolves would first scatter, then isolate, and finally devour at will every member of the flock of the Good Shepherd. Thank God, or hallelujah, for the community of the faithful!

January 18

"I saw in the
right hand of him that
sat on the throne a book
written within and on
the backside, sealed
with seven seals."
(Revelation 5:1).

Just
as those who
are addicted to drugs
keep coming back for one
more fix, the wicked continue
to demand signs from the ministers
of the Lord as proof of their authority.
Those with adulterous hearts seek signs
for the satisfaction of desires that require an
increasing intensity of validation for the same
levels of gratification. But, at times, signs are
given for no reason other than to vindicate
prophetic warning. Because consequences
naturally follows actions, signs may be
given to establish our accountability.
In any event, the wicked are left
with responsibility for their
indefensible behavior,
regardless of their
acceptance or
rejection of
signs.

January 19

"I saw
an angel come
down from heaven,
having the key of the
bottomless pit and a great
chain in his hand."
(Revelation 20:1).

"Death is not
extinguishing a light;
it is putting out the lamp
because the dawn has come."
(R. Tagore). It is self-evident that
we were born to die, but those with
childlike faith will "not taste of death,
for it shall be sweet unto them." (D&C
42:47). Thou shalt live together in love,"
taught the Savior, "insomuch that thou
shalt weep for the loss of them that die,
and more especially for those that have
not hope of a glorious resurrection."
(D&C 42:45). To a world spiritually
illiterate, Latter-day Saints "give
great lessons in the grammar of
the gospel, including this one:
death is a mere comma, not
an exclamation point."
(Neal A. Maxwell).

January 20

"And his sweat was, as it were, great drops of blood falling down to the ground." (Luke 22:44).

Nephi correctly taught that "it is by grace that we are saved, after all we can do." (2 Nephi 25:23). Latter-day Saints, however, tend to emphasize works to the point that it may seem to others that the grace of God takes a back seat to their own efforts to earn salvation. In spite of our preoccupation with agency, accountability, industry, and labor, as we urge each other to a greater sense of our duty, devotion, and diligence, the truth is that nothing we can do will qualify us to enjoy eternal life. It is only in the blood of the Lord and Savior Jesus Christ, and through His sacrifice and His redeeming grace, that we are rescued from our carnal nature and fallen state that is the enemy of God.

January 21

"Behold,
there are save two
churches only. The one is
the church of the Lamb of
God, and the other is the
church of the devil."
(1 Nephi 14:10).

The wicked are
able to feel neither loyalty
nor love for anything or anyone
but themselves, and they enjoy neither
the blessings of unity nor the peace that is
the province solely of the righteous. They are
bound by the father of contention, who oversees
the self-destruction of his children and perversely
enjoys the process. Those who belong to his church
are punished by their sins, and not so much for them.
We think that it is God Who applies punishment, and
that He does it externally, the way parents often do,
but He does not. They may say: "If you don't clean
up your room, you can't drive the car for a week."
But God says, "If you don't clean up your room,
you'll have to live in it for a week." We must
endure the consequences of our violation of
eternal law, that have been handcrafted
by our all-wise Father to address the
needs that have been dictated by
our individual circumstances;
that we might be properly
motivated to amend our
errant behavior.

January 22

"He
hath
brought
us into this
place, and hath
given us this land,
even a land that floweth
with milk and honey."
(Deuteronomy 26:9).

It is only after we have
tried the virtue of the word
of God, that can we know that
he "doth grant unto (us) whatsoever
(we) ask that is right, in faith, believing
that (we) shall receive. O then, how (we)
ought to impart of the substance that (we)
have, one to another." (Mosiah 4:21). The
church offers us wonderful opportunities
for our practice of an active, meaningful
brotherhood. An institutional welfare,
on the other hand, generally offers
only detached, disinterested, and
disconnected paternalism, all
with an economic baseline
that either trivializes or
ignores the intrinsic
worth of souls.

January 23

"And out of
the ground made the
Lord God to grow every
tree that is pleasant to the
sight, and good for food;
the tree of life also in the
midst of the garden, and
the tree of knowledge
of good and evil."
(Genesis 2:17).

In the
symbolism
of the tree of life,
we see the reflection
of the love of God. Its fruit,
as expected, represents eternal
life, which is the greatest gift our
Father could give His children. There
are many who are actively, passionately,
and desperately fighting their way through
swirling mists of darkness as they make their
way to the tree of life and its precious fruit. In
Nephi's account, those who arrived at the tree
fell down at its base, completely spent as a
result of their efforts. A new meaning is
given to Alma's expression of being
"swallowed up in the joy of (our)
God, even to the exhausting
of (our) strength."
(Alma 27:17).

January 24

"The kingdom of heaven is like unto a merchant man, seeking godly pearls, who, when he had found one pearl of great price, went and sold all that he had, and bought it." (Matthew 13:45-46).

Harold B. Lee said: "The receding horizons of life ever mock the attempts at acquisition and conquest of those who are ambitious for personal gain and personal advantage." Our efforts are best expended when they result in spiritual fitness or health. Our testimony of the gospel and its exalting principles never comes as an unearned gift. The Savior said: "Behold, you have not understood," for "you have supposed that I would give it unto you, when you took no thought save it was to ask me, But, behold, I say unto you, that you must study it out in your mind." (D&C 9:7-8). Agency, that at its best gives us the power to make correct choices, is not free. It is purchased at a substantial cost. Perhaps it would be better to characterize it as free will, or even as freedom of expression, rather than as 'free agency,' which it certainly is not.

January 25

"Enter ye in at
the strait gate. For
wide is the gate, and
broad is the way, that
leadeth to destruction."
(Matthew 7:13).

Within the parameters
of God's "Great and Eternal Plan of
Deliverance from Death," (2 Nephi 11:5),
there can be no latitude in the provision that
states that He "cannot look upon sin with the least
degree of allowance." (D&C 1:31). Thus, there is no
alternative to baptism; it typifies the portal through
which we must all pass on our journey home to the
celestial courts of God. Faith and repentance lead
us to that narrow gate, on whose far side lie the
remission of sins, membership in the church,
as well as sanctification through receipt of
the Holy Ghost. The way is strait and the
standard undeviating, with no room for
rationalization or compromise. There
can be no allowance made for the
indifferent substitution of less
rigorous stipulations that
attempt to homogenize
the requirements for
forgiveness of
our sins.

January 26

"I have set thee for a tower and a fortress among my people, that thou mayest know and try their way."
(Jeremiah 6:27).

At the Bar of Justice, some will persistently press a point that has been stubbornly advocated by those who are doctrinally misinformed. They will argue that there were many equally acceptable paths leading to the Kingdom of God. They will ask if it matters so much whether they had been a Quaker, a Methodist, or an Evangelical. They will posit the view that as long as they had accepted the Lord, invoked His name, and given Him the credit for personal accomplishments, all could not have been in vain. We all need to understand the literal meaning of Paul's revelatory statement that there is only "one Lord, one faith, and one baptism."
(Ephesians 4:5-6).

January 27

"Every
man may act
in doctrine and
principle pertaining
to futurity, according to
the moral agency which
I have given unto him,
that every man may
be accountable for
for his own sins
in the day of
judgment."
(D&C 101:78).

"I've never
given my agency
to anyone except Christ,"
said Boyd Packer, "and I want
you to know that the experience was
akin to Gethsemane." So too, when we give
ourselves completely and without reservation
to the Savior, to the only One who is mighty
to save, when we have been born again, not
through maturation, but by generation, it
is sometimes a harrowing ordeal. We
experience a refining process, as the
white-hot cauldron over a divine
fire purges the disposition to
sin from the marrow of our
bones. If we can't stand
the heat, we should
get out of the
kitchen.

January 28

"And
the angel
of the Lord
appeared unto
him in a flame of
fire out of the midst of
a bush. And he looked,
and, behold, the bush
burned with fire, and
the bush was not
consumed."
(Exodus 3:2).

Israel was
drawn to Eastern
mysticism just as moths
are attracted to fire, and she
was mesmerized by its worldly
manifestations, even though it was
only an illusion and a caricature of the
tremendous power symbolized by the
burning bush. Sinai, after all is said, is
an attitude more than it is a place. The
faithful and true loose the latchets of
their sandals because they realize
that holy sanctuaries have been
designed to be a part of their
daily experience, and are
ever before their
face.

January 29

"The Lord shall have
power over his saints and
shall reign in their midst, and
shall come down in judgment
upon Idumea," that is to
say, "the world."
(D&C 1:36).

Lucifer,
a son of the
morning, was cast out
of heaven for his rebellion,
because he could not abide by
the principles that governed the
lives of his brothers and sisters, who
were nurtured within the warm embrace
of their Father. He became Satan, who now
rules in Idumea, or the world. The Saints must
choose their allegiance, because they cannot hold
membership in both the assembly of God and the
Great and Abominable Church of the Devil. They
cannot hope to live in Zion, while maintaining
a summer home in Babylon, any more than
they can afford to joy ride through the
world, making excuses to stop
along the way to partake of
its pleasures and taste
its tempting
treats.

January 30

"Let no
man deceive
you by any means.
For that day shall not
come, except there come a
falling away first, and that
man of sin be revealed,
the son of perdition."
(2 Thessalonians 2:3).

"The
religion builders" of
our day "have so distorted
and deformed the doctrines of
Jesus, so muffled them in mysticisms,
fancies and falsehoods, have caricatured
them into forms so inconceivable, as to shock
reasonable thinkers. Happy in the prospect of
a restoration of primitive Christianity, I must
leave it to younger persons to encounter and
lop off the false branches which have been
grafted into it by the mythologists of
the middle and modern ages."
(Thomas Jefferson).

January 31

"And behold I say unto you all that this was a snare of the adversary, which he has laid to catch this people, that he might bring you into subjection unto him, that he might encircle you about with his chains," and drag you down to hell, to destruction.
(Alma 12:6).

Father, may I never forget to call upon Thee to protect me from worldly influences, and from that old serpent Beelzebub. I know that Satan is abroad in the land, for I hear his siren call coming from Babylon, ringing loudly in my ears.

February 1

As they draw
near to the Judgment
Bar "the righteous shall
have a perfect knowledge
of their enjoyment, and their
righteousness, being clothed
with purity...even with the
robe of righteousness."
(2 Nephi 9:14).

Gandhi,
"the great soul,"
proclaimed a simple
statement of belief that has
changed forever how we look
at both ourselves and the world:
"My life," he said, "is my message."
He was faithful to his principles, the
moral and ethical constants that were
as guiding stars leading him to safety.
The Savior, Who is our Exemplar, was
as a Prototype of the perfection that is
within our reach. Without His divine
intervention, though, we would be
doomed to failure in our efforts to
be as He is. His gospel is the key
element that breaks down every
barrier that stands in the way
of our personal progress. It
is the law of liberty in a
world where attacks
on our freedom are
becoming more
common.

February 2

David
told Goliath,
who stood before
him: "Thou comest to
me with a sword, and with
a spear, and with a shield, but I
come to thee in the name of the
Lord of hosts, the God of the
armies of Israel, whom thou
hast defied. This day will
the Lord deliver thee
into mine hand."
(1 Samuel 17:45).

When
Lamanite ruffians
came to scatter the flocks
of King Lamoni, Ammon had
unbridled confidence in the power
of God. Therefore, he anticipated with
joy a situation that, at the same time, must
have caused palpitations in the hearts of his
fearful companions. Today, we too must face our
own "Lamanites by the Waters of Sebus." All of us
have similar needs, but the primary focus of our
shared concern should be on the preservation
of our eternal lives. In truth, proper prior
preparation, and an abiding confidence
in God's power, will prevent the poor
performance of our priesthood
profession in the very hour
of our greatest need.

February 3

"I call
heaven and
earth to record
this day against you,
that I have set before you
life and death, blessing and
cursing. Therefore choose
life, that both thou and
thy seed may live."
(Deuteronomy 30:19).

There
is a clear and
unambiguous choice
that every single child of
God has been blessed to face in
this life. It is not between poverty
and wealth, nor is it between sickness
and health, or happiness and misery, or
between fame and obscurity The choice is
between good and evil. And so, when Jesus
comes again, His glory will be like a fire that
purges out all of the accumulated impurities
of blemished lives. Following the process of
refining, if imperfections remain, metal is
without value. Good for nothing, it must
be cast upon the scrap heap. Only if it
has been cleansed of contamination,
can it be fashioned into a thing of
value that will stand up under
punishing use, and with the
respect it has earned, give
years of consistently
reliable service.

February 4

None
"shall hurt
nor destroy
in all my holy
mountain, for the
earth shall be full of
the knowledge of the
Lord, as the waters
cover the sea."
(Isaiah 11:9).

Many times in the
holy scriptures, the prophets
utilized the word "mountain" both
allegorically and figuratively, to refer to
a high place of God, a place of revelation, and
perhaps to the temple of the Lord. In some cases it
refers to Mount Zion, or Jerusalem. In the Last Days,
"the Lord's house will be established in the tops of the
mountains." (Isaiah 2:2) This may be a reference to
the intermountain west, but that interpretation
may be too narrow, because the Lord warned
Joseph Smith: "Let them who be of Judah
flee unto the mountains of the Lord's
house." (D&C 133:13). Clearly, the
eternal city of Jerusalem must
be considered when this
scripture is being
interpreted.

February 5

"And
I will shew
wonders in heaven
above, and signs in
the earth beneath;
blood, and fire,
and vapour
of smoke."
(Acts 2:19).

When
the conduct
of our lives seem to
be going well, we are often
fooled into thinking that we can
control events and determine outcomes,
when, in fact, most are beyond our influence.
What we can control is our creative and adaptive
response to the unpredictable circumstances that are
a part of our daily lives. We will not then be as children
who have been tossed to and fro, as flotsam and jetsam on
the sea of life, and who are "carried about with every wind
of doctrine, by the sleight of men, and cunning craftiness."
(Ephesians 4:14). There are those living among us who
stand for nothing but will fall for anything, and who
think very little of cursing the darkness without
ever stopping to light a candle. They lack a
strong will, but make up for it with an
even more powerful won't. If they
bend their knee, they only do
so because they think they
are taking a bow.

February 6

"They
profess
that they
know God,
but in works
they deny him,
being abominable
and disobedient,
and unto every
good work
reprobate."
(Titus 1:16).

Secular Christianity is abominable, and its mission has been corrupted, because it subtly and craftily leads the children of God away from the truth. Without their conscious realization, it stops their progression by destroying the very purpose of mortality in the great Plan of Salvation. Insult is added to injury when hypocrisy further perverts doctrine into humanized, spiritually impotent dogma, when they do not really believe, but are only professors of religion. Such have been labeled by the Lord as imposters, who "draw near to Him with their lips, but whose hearts are far from Him. Those who are substantively no more than 'professors of religion' are those who "teach for doctrines the commandments of men." They have "a form of godliness, but they deny the power thereof."
(J.S.H. 1:19).

February 7

In the
heavens, before
time itself existed,
"God spared not the
angels that sinned, but
cast them down to hell,
and delivered them into
chains of darkness, to
be reserved unto
judgment."
(2 Peter 2:4).

It seems to
be inevitable that
when hearts have been
hardened and minds have been
closed to the message of salvation
that is proclaimed by the Lord's servants,
the light of truth is diminished as the Spirit is
withdrawn. The point is finally reached, when those
wretched souls, concentered all in self, are left without
defense against the relentlessly aggressive tactics of
the devil. Because they rely solely upon their own
resources, they are influenced more by the lies of
the deceiver than by the illuminating truths of
the Spirit. They are dragged by the heavy
weight of the chains of darkness, down
to a living hell manifest by confusion
and misunderstanding, and by an
ignorance that sows the seeds of
despair, and is oppressively,
inexorably, and ruthlessly
self-destructive.

February 8

"Search the
scriptures, for ye
think that in them ye
have eternal life, and
they are they which
testify of me."
(John 5:39).

If it were possible to
bring together all the written
records from our past, we would find
that, overwhelmingly, they are "religious
in nature; that the primary purpose to which
writing has been put thru the ages has been for
keeping a remembrance of God's dealing with
men." (Hugh Nibley). A striking exception to
this rule has been the profusion of profane
propaganda pouring out from the press
in the past 200 years, like an avalanche.
Satan's secular humanists have at last
found a forum for falsehood in both
print and electronic media. Little
wonder that Jacob warned us
that to be learned is good,
but only if we hearken
to the counsel of
God.

February 9

"We
have also a more
sure word of prophecy
whereunto ye do well that
ye take heed, as unto a light
that shineth in a dark place,
until the day dawn, and
the day star arise in
your hearts."
(2 Peter 1:19).

The
image of
heaven "lies
about us in our
infancy. Shades of
the prison-house begin
to close upon the growing
boy, but behold, he sees the
light, and whence it flows. He
sees it in his joy. The youth, who
daily farther from the east must
travel, still is nature's priest, and
by the vision splendid, is on his
way attended. At length, the
man perceives it die away,
and fade into the light
of common day."
(Wordsworth).

February 10

"Thou
hast been
in Eden, the
garden of God."
(Ezekiel 28:13).

In the
real world, we
grip our faith tightly,
and hang on for the ride. We
listen closely, and almost hear the
Spirit whisper: "All these things shall
give thee experience." Then, we let our
love for the Lord cast out all fear and we
move forward because we know that His
perspective is wider and clearer than any
caricature that has been fashioned by the
world's manipulation and distortion of
images of our former home. It was for
our own good that we were driven
from a morally static environment
into unfamiliar territory that was
dangerous, but was filled with
unimaginable opportunity. In
the lone and dreary world,
living by the sweat of our
brow is not punishment,
but is a celebratory
experience.

February 11

"He drove out the man; and he
placed at the east of the garden of
Eden cherubims, and a flaming
sword which turned every
way, to keep the way
of the tree of life."
(Genesis 13:24).

It is beyond
the comprehension
of the faithless that each of
us came into the world that we
might die. Surely, before we left our
pre-mortal home, we must have clearly
understood that the Plan of Salvation would
require the death of our bodies. Adam was sent
to dwell with Eve in Eden with the understanding
that he would violate or transgress a law in order
to live and then to die. After his fall from grace,
cherubim were instructed by God to prevent
Adam from inappropriately partaking
of the fruit of the Tree of Life before
first being taught the principles
of the Plan of Happiness. Had
he done so, he and Eve
would have lived
forever in their
sins.

February 12

"Ye were
without Christ,
being aliens from the
commonwealth of Israel, and
strangers from the covenants of
promise, having no hope,"
since ye were "without
God in the world."
(Ephesians 2:12).

Those
who have seized the
opportunity to enter into a
covenant relationship with God
are they "who have come out of the
world, who have left the loneliness and
the estrangement of a fallen creation and
entered into the realm of divine experience.
They have forsaken the orphanage of spiritual
alienation and been received into the family and
household of the Lord Jesus Christ. They have left
the ranks of the nameless and have taken upon
themselves the blessed name of Jesus Christ.
They are Christians. Through their Master,
they will become, in time, joint heirs
of all that the Father has."
(Robert L. Millet).

February 13

"As
the fire
devoureth
the stubble, and
the flame consumeth
the chaff, so their root
shall be as rottenness, and
their blossom shall go up as
dust, because they have cast
away the law of the Lord of
hosts, and (have) despised
the word of the Holy
One of Israel."
(Isaiah 5:24).

When
people turn
their backs on the
Law, their temporal
preparation will be of
no benefit in avoiding the
pitfalls to progression and
inevitable disasters that will
rain down upon the nations.
The approaching calamity is
symbolized by the burning
of both stubble and chaff,
that are very quickly
engulfed, and then
consumed by
fire.

February 14

"Every idle word that they shall speak they shall give account thereof in the day of judgment. For by thy words thou shalt be justified, and by thy words, thou shalt be condemned."
(Matthew 12:36-37).

Murmuring is perhaps best described as the subdued and continually repeated expression of indistinct or inarticulate complaints. Sometimes, it is the mutated form of grumbling about things with which we are not happy. As an earthquake, murmuring can build into harmonic waves with the power to undermine the foundation of relationships and institutions. Murmurers expect results without responsibility, and so, theirs is a cowardly act. Although it is often conducted anonymously within the cloak of secrecy, its effect is felt publicly. Those who murmur want a tangible return without having made a legitimate investment.

February 15

"And the
mists of darkness
are the temptations of the
devil, which blindeth the eyes, and
hardeneth the hearts of the children
of men, and leadeth them away
into broad roads, that they
perish and are lost."
(1 Nephi 12:17).

As
we begin to
move along the
path leading back to
heaven, we must press
forward with purpose. It is
not enough that we have been
baptized and have received the
Spirit. We cannot camp out on the
path by remaining in a passive, or a
morally static, state. The only person
who every had his work done for him
by Friday was Robinson Crusoe. Thus,
the Lord's rejection of "many (who) will
say to (Him) in that day: Lord, Lord,
have we not…in thy name done
many wonderful works?"
(3 Nephi 14:22).

February 16

"Thou shalt put in the breastplate of judgment the Urim and the Thummim."
(Exodus 28:30).

Religion itself often becomes magical when the power of the church is transferred from God to those who profess to be His earthly representatives, but who are, in reality, only competing for market share. Priesthood acquires the status of an office mechanically bestowing both blessings and grace, regardless of the moral or spiritual qualifications of its possessor. The Bible then appears to convey power and knowledge without the need for revelation. Moroni saw that there would be many in the Last Days who had "transfigured the holy word of God," or who had 'wrested' the scriptures, changing their appearance and their substance to meet their profane needs. (Mormon 8:33).

February 17

"For the Lord shall comfort Zion. He will comfort all her waste places; and he will make her wilderness like Eden, and her desert like the garden of the Lord; joy and gladness shall be found therein, thanksgiving, and the voice of melody." (Isaiah 51:3).

We should have unbridled confidence in God's promise that we will find joy by living gospel-centered lives. It is not the result of our wishful thinking, nor is it our misguided trust in promises that have no reasonable expectation of fulfillment. It is not a high stakes gamble based on a statistical improbability. It is the inevitable reward of well-founded faith in God, after having mastered the discipline to control our desires and emotions within the boundaries that He has set; when our priorities harmonize with the doctrines of the kingdom and the principles of the gospel. Our actions reflect His noble character, and they speak louder than our words because they paint a portrait of a God-centered earth that is a shared sensory experience.

February 18

"The cow
and the bear
shall feed. Their
young ones shall
lie down together;
and the lion shall eat
straw like the ox."
(Isaiah 11:7).

Employing the melodic poetry of metaphor that has a familiar ring to those who love his writing style, Isaiah described what life will be like during the Millennium. He painted a portrait of a God-centered society where faithfulness triumphs, and "the earth (is) full of the knowledge of the Lord, as the waters cover the sea." (Isaiah 11:9). Brigham Young declared: When righteousness dictates the conduct of millennial culture, the earth itself will also be sanctified. With the Spirit of God, "every animal and creeping thing will be filled with peace; the soil of the earth will bring forth in its strength, and the fruits thereof will be meat for man. The more purity that exists, the less is the strife; the more kind we are to our animals, the more will peace increase, and the savage nature of the brute creation will vanish away."

February 19

"The kingdom of heaven is like
unto a treasure hid in a field, the
which when a man hath found, he
hideth, and for joy thereof goeth
and selleth all that he hath,
and buyeth that field."
(Matthew 13:44).

When Lehi's sons
returned to Jerusalem to
retrieve the Plates of Brass,
that were the written records of
their family, they traced their way
back to their home on the outskirts of
the city, and gathered up all the treasures
they had left behind. These they presented to
Laban, to whom they were offered in exchange
for the precious things they really valued. But the
Lord did not allow them to receive the spiritual gift
of the scriptures in exchange for the profane baubles
and ornaments of the world. Ultimately, at the hands
of their unscrupulous cousin, they lost their telestial
trinkets so that the Lord might thereafter prove to
them that He was mightier than man, saw the
end from the beginning, and was firmly
in control of not only their temporal,
but also their spiritual destiny.
Never again would Nephi
doubt that the Lord
would provide.

February 20

"Where your
treasure is, there will
your heart be also."
(Matthew 6:21).

Those
who suffer from
a weakness in their
character are often defined
by temporal trappings that are
simply distractions from the intangible
substance that is at the core of our existence.
They may weave ecclesiastical embroidery into
the coat of many colors that was envisioned to be the
foundation garment of a heavenly wardrobe. These may
simply be improvised accouterments, or nothing more than
doctrinal decorations that have been hastily designed to prop
up faltering faith. Self-actualized church members, on the other
hand, take their cues from the inside. The source of their power
lies, not only in their dreams, ideals, and values, but also in their
core operating principles. These are not readily influenced by
external pressures, and so, are not easily subject to change.
Their healthy reliance upon the tender mercies of Christ
provides just the balance they need, and gives them an
exhilarating vision of their potential to become self-
directed, self-managed, and self-motivated, all
within the parameters of a perfect Plan
wherein they can be guided and
mentored by God.

February 21

"He hath
blinded their eyes
and hardened their
hearts, that they should
not see with their eyes, nor
understand with their heart
and be converted, that I
should heal them."
(John 12:40).

Ironically,
the standard of the
blind who lead the blind
is "seeing is believing," but
seeing is not only irrelevant in the
acquisition of faith, but it also conveys
the wrong message. Those who question
the faith and testimony of the Saints are the
living proof of the Great Apostasy. For them,
it has not yet ended. Faith, however, is the
spiritual strong searchlight that allows
the disciples of Christ to fearlessly
step into the darkness, that they
might exercise their trust in
God as they petition Him
to illuminate the path
that stretches out
before them.

February 22

In
the Last Days,
Israel "shall say no
more the fathers have
eaten a sour grape, and
the children's teeth
are set on edge."
(Jeremiah 31:29).

Adversity, that is
so much a part of our
lives can be either a diamond
dust polishing us to a high luster,
or it can be the abrasive that wears us
down as it grinds us to pieces. However,
we cannot hope to effectively deal with our
difficulties without having first focused our
lives on Jesus Christ. As He taught: "If men
come unto me, I will show unto them their
weakness. I give unto men weakness that
they may be humble; and my grace is
sufficient for all men that humble
themselves before me; for if they
humble themselves before me,
and have faith in me, then
will I make weak things
strong unto them."
(Ether 12:27).

February 23

For all who
stare in wide-
eyed wonder, "the
heavens declare the
glory of God, and the
firmament sheweth
his handiwork."
(Psalms 19:1).

The sum
of our existence
just may be anchored
to an infinite hierarchy of
universes, "organized into the
equivalent of galaxies and smaller
structures, and an immense number of
much tinier elementary particles, which
are universes at the next level, and so on
in an infinitely downward regression of
universes within universes, endlessly;
and upward as well. What, I wonder,
would the other universes be like?"
(Carl Sagan, "Cosmos"). Who can
say? Even now, we are poised at
the edge of forever, ready to
jump off into eternity. God
will open our eyes soon
enough, and when He
does, we shall see
things as they
really are.

February 24

"They glorified Him not as God, neither were thankful, but became vain in their imaginations." (Romans 1:21).

Our actions are "in vain" when they have no value; when they are worthless. For example, "to try in vain" is to struggle without the expectation of success. Taking the name of the Lord "in vain" is blasphemous because it is using His name improperly and without authority. Those who do so are imposters, invoking the name of Deity in a false, misleading, and counterfeit way. So too, sinful behavior is vain. It is caving in to pressure to follow the path of least resistance. It is doing one thing, when something else of far greater consequence could have been accomplished with just a little more blood, soul sweat, and tears. It is settling for mediocrity rather than following the more difficult road that leads to greater heights. It is a capitulation to spiritual stagnation rather than acceptance of the effort required to surmount obstacles in the quest for enlightenment. It is akin to trading our eternal birthright for a mess of pottage.

February 25

"Proclaim ye this
among the Gentiles.
Prepare war, wake up the
mighty men, let all the men
of war draw near… Beat your
plowshares into swords and
your pruning hooks into
spears. Let the weak
say, I am strong."
(Joel 3:9-10).

Because the word
of God is foreign to the petty
pleading of the adversary, those who
lack spiritual strength often resort to violence
in a vain attempt to bolster their position. But power
and violence are mutually exclusive; where one is present
the other is absent. Those who are least prepared for positions
of trust and responsibility seem to be those who are the most
inclined to abuse authority. Measured against the standard
of heaven, power is a poor substitute for leadership, and
is antithetical to real authority It is a violation of
the law of the Celestial Kingdom to engage in
hostility or to abrogate the rights of others
behind the cloak of a supposed
exercise of temporal
power.

February 26

"Give not that
which is holy unto the
dogs, neither cast ye your
pearls before swine, lest they
trample them under their
feet, and turn again
and rend you."
(Matthew 7:6).

The
seraphim
who surrounded
God's throne cried one
"unto another, and said:
Holy, holy, holy is the Lord
of Hosts; and the whole earth is
full of his glory." (2 Nephi 16:2).
In Hebrew, to repeat something
three times makes it superlative,
as in "good," "better," and "best."
These fiery beings, in support of
a celestial Superstar, desired to
make the bold statement, that
in all of creation there can be
no Being that is more holy
than the Firstborn of the
Father, "a lamb without
blemish and without
or spot." (1 Peter
1:19).

February 27

"Thrust in your
sickle with all your soul,
and your sins are forgiven
you, and you shall be laden
with sheaves upon your
back, for the laborer is
worthy of his hire."
(D&C 31:10).

We
must never
allow ourselves to
squander our resources,
or to waste precious energy
in a preoccupation with what is
missing. Focusing our attention on
what we lack can become a paralyzing
fear. That flawed strategy will ultimately
defeat us. Instead, we need to concentrate on
the assets that are available to us, be they large
or small, capitalize on them, and turn them
into forces for positive, substantive, and
significant change. We must pray as if
everything depended upon the will
of God, as it surely does, but then
get to work, as if the ultimate
success of our joint venture
with Him rested upon
our own initiative or
determination.

February 28

"And he had
in his right hand
seven stars; and out of
his mouth went a sharp
two edged sword; and his
countenance was as the sun
(that) shineth in his strength."
(Revelation 1:16).

"Ye are
no more strangers
and foreigners, but fellow
citizens with the saints, and of the
household of God." (Ephesians 2:19). The
recipients of Paul's epistle were congregants of
one of the seven churches in Asia, who might have
seen themselves as privileged members of an exclusive
ecclesiastical country club situated on a narrow theological
terrace. They may have been accustomed to giving each other
high-fives and gracious compliments, while at the same time
treating those outside their inner circle in a deprecating way.
But Paul directed that, should strangers from Sardis, Smyrna,
Philadelphia, or Pergamum, or foreigners from Thyatira or
Laodicea arrive in Ephesus, they were to be welcomed in
the bonds of fellowship, and to be warmly received by
the Saints into the household of God. They were
not to be mistreated as undocumented illegal
immigrants, or as if they were on a "no
fly" watch list of subversives, that
was maintained by the local
authorities.

February 29

"Before the throne
there was a sea of glass
like unto crystal, and in the
midst of the throne…were
four beasts full of eyes
before and behind."
(Revelation 4:6).

We risk relaxing,
distorting, or losing our
firm grip on reality when we
crowd ourselves into conceptual
cul-de-sacs, religious roundabouts, and
doctrinal dead ends from which there is no easy
avenue of escape. A one-dimensional person with a
narrow view of the world will perceive things not as they
really are, but only as their limited vision permits them to
see. The gospel perspective gives us a multi-dimensional
view of existence that provides a much more accurate
representation of our surroundings. In this sense,
the glory of God is intelligence, or the ability to
perceive and process information relating to
the physical and spiritual worlds around
us, even the multi-dimensional world
that is our native environment, in
spite of the fact that it cannot
be seen with our natural
eyes.

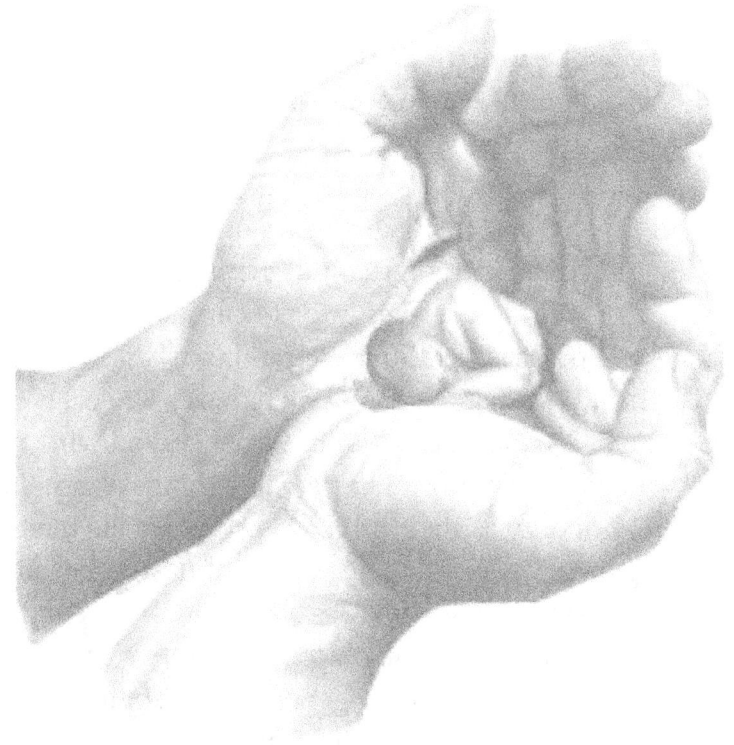

March 1

"I would
not that ye should
be ignorant, how that all
our fathers...did all drink the
same spiritual drink. For they
drank of that spiritual Rock
that followed them, and
that Rock was Christ."
(1 Corinthians 10:1 & 4).

The
undeniable
consciousness of
victory over ourselves
and of our communion with
the infinite is the hallmark of our
spirituality. The terrifying jungle of
worldliness is always close at hand, but
we cannot allow ourselves to compromise
our standards and yield to the siren song of
Satan's seductive sentinels. Ours must always
be the non-negotiable standard of the celestial
bound disciple. We must be firm and resolute,
for as Alexander Pope pointed out, the risks
of accommodation can be high, for vice
is "a monster of so frightful mien, as
to be hated needs but to be seen.
Yet seen too oft, familiar with
her face, we first endure,
then pity, then
embrace."

March 2

"The fir trees rejoice
at thee, and the cedars of
Lebanon, saying: Since
thou art laid down,
no feller is come
up against us."
(Isaiah 14:8).

The
mountains of
Lebanon were once
shaded by vast forests that
have been described as "the
Cedars of God." The trees must
have been a sight for those with sore
eyes. They were evergreen and beautiful,
with wide-spreading branches whose shade
provided rest for the weary, and their wood was
pleasantly aromatic. They were long-lived and had
many uses. The prophets have characterized members
of the church as cedars of Lebanon, who will declare that
since the destruction of Babylon, no feller, or person who
cuts down trees, has come up against them to smite them.
As a matter of fact, the righteous shall instead "flourish
like the palm tree (and) grow like a cedar in Lebanon.
Those that be planted in the house of the Lord shall
flourish in the courts of our God." (Psalms 92:12).
Trees often grow in what appear to be desert
wastes. It is only on closer inspection that
the oasis of an underlying current of
life-sustaining water is noticed,
that brings nourishment
to the roots of the
thirsty plants.

March 3

Just two years
after the organization
of the church, the Saints, and in
particular Bishop Edward Partridge, were
warned that, even though they had been called
and appointed to specific area of responsibility,
they must not put forth their hands "to steady
the ark of God." Even if their intentions were
without guile, they would "fall by the shaft
of death, like as a tree that is smitten by
the vivid shaft of lightning."
(D&C 85:8).

All
who bear
the vessels of
the Lord must be
clean. Anciently, the
ark was a tangible object
that symbolized the presence
of God, His throne, His glory, as
well as His divine majesty. Only the
High Priest who was a type of Christ
could approach it, and then only after
going through an elaborate ritual of
personal cleansing and propitiation
for his sins. The holiness of God is
emphasized in the scriptures. No
unclean thing can ever hope to
exist in His presence, for it is
an everlasting burning like
a refining fire that licks
up and consumes
impurity.

March 4

"Take
thee one
stick, and write
upon it, for Judah,
and for the children
of Israel his companions;
then take another stick, and
write upon it, for Joseph, the
stick of Ephraim, and for
all the house of Israel
his companions."
(Ezekiel 37:16).

Nothing short of the plain
and most precious teachings of
the Lord and Savior Jesus Christ can
explain the special covenant relationship
that Israel has always enjoyed with its God.
(See 1 Nephi 13:26).These truths are even more
clearly understood in The Book of Mormon than
they are in the Bible, "wherefore they shall both be
established in one." (1 Nephi 13:41). Through the Law
of Witnesses, these two books will confirm the divinity
of our Redeemer. "That which shall be written" in the
Bible and The Book of Mormon "shall grow together,
unto the confounding of false doctrines and laying
down of contentions," and establishing an era of
peace among the tribes of the House of Israel,
by "bringing them to a knowledge of my
covenants, saith the Lord," for He has
always been, and forever will be,
their one and only God.
(2 Nephi 3:12).

March 5

"But thus
saith the Lord,
even the captives
of the mighty shall
be taken away, and the
prey of the terrible shall be
delivered. For I will contend
with him that contendeth
with thee, and I will
save thy children."
(Isaiah 49:25).

Every
single one of the
children of God who
has been miraculously
liberated from their telestial
bondage, who sees in sudden
sunbursts of spiritual sensitivity
that Jesus Christ is the Light of the
world, needs friends in the church,
a responsibility, and to be nourished
by the good word of God. As Joseph
Smith beseeched the Saints: "Brethren,
shall we not go on in so great a cause?
Courage, brethren; and on, on to the
victory! Let your hearts rejoice,
and be exceedingly glad."
(D&C 128:22).

March 6

"Lord, hedge
not up my way,
but the ways of
mine enemy."
(2 Nephi 4:33).

Only
after we have
cleared our heads,
are we able to zoom
in, as it were, with our
mind's eye, to give our most
important objectives clarity that
is crystal clear. Then, enlightenment
thru the Spirit flows in one of the most
pure forms of focus. It allows input from
the five somatic senses to be transformed
by our spiritual sixth sense to structure an
appropriate hierarchy of value. After we
have been conditioned by our diligence,
faith, and patience, information of the
highest priority will automatically be
given immediate attention. We may
then draw upon both our spiritual
and natural resources to address
the concerns that, as Winston
Churchill said, demand not
only our blood and our
toil, but also our
tears, and our
sweat.

March 7

"Whosoever shall compel
thee to go a mile, go
with him twain."
(Matthew 5:41).

Even if
you're on the
right road, you're
going to get run over if
you just sit there. Work and
idleness are incompatible. There
is a world of difference between the
"cheap thrills" that are so often the focus
of attention of the idler, and the "lofty goals"
of the working man. Frequently, our problem is
not that we set our goals too high, and fail to reach
them. It is, instead, that we set them too low, and we
do reach them far too easily. If we mistakenly confuse
our mediocrity for well-deserved success, we become
conditioned to accept only our marginal effort as the
standard to which we should aspire. Little wonder
that the Lord has said "the idler shall not have
place in the church." (D&C 75:29). He does
not follow the example of the world by
handing out plastic participation
trophies to everyone who
has merely shown
up for class.

March 8

"He
that
findeth
his life shall
lose it, and he that
loseth his life for my
sake shall find it."
(Matthew 10:39).

When we have made
covenants with God, only to
then conspicuously compromise the
standard to which we have pledged our
undeviating allegiance, we may thereafter
"wax strong in wickedness and abominations."
(3 Nephi 2:3). It is one thing for an ignorant people
to live in opposition to the laws of God, but it is quite
another for those who have had the light to turn from it,
willfully rebel, and consciously seek an alternative path of
darkness. That is a course of action which is an abomination,
because it represents unfaithfulness to God. It is not easy for
those who repudiate His gifts to obtain forgiveness. Those
who perish in such circumstances must die in their sins.
They cannot be saved in God's kingdom.
(See Moroni 10:26).

March 9

"Now these
mysteries are not
yet fully made known
unto me, therefore,
I shall forbear."
(Alma 37:11).

Perhaps it will
come as a surprise to
some, to learn that there
still exist doctrines relating to
the expansive scope of the Plan of
Salvation that simply have not yet been
made clear, either in the scriptures, or in the
teachings of the prophets. Alma felt that it was
always better to keep his opinion to himself, rather
than to speculate without a foundation of revelation.
It is prudent, he suggested, that one remain silent and
be thought a fool, than to speak, and remove all doubt
in the matter. When counseling his son Corianton, he
underscored this point: "There are many mysteries."
he explained, "which are kept, that no one knoweth
them, save God himself." (Alma 40:3). He taught
that when God withholds understanding from
His children, it is "for a wise purpose," and
there has been no intent to mislead or to
deceive. We can always be certain
that "his paths are straight."
(Alma 40:12).

March 10

"The light of the body is the eye. If, therefore, thine eye be single, thy whole body shall be full of light." (Matthew 6:22).

We are far richer today than we were yesterday, if we have shared our smile, laughed often, given something, but forgiven even more, changed stumbling blocks into stepping stones, or made a new friend; or if we have thought more in terms of thyself than ourselves, if we have managed to be cheerful even when we were weary, if we have received His image in our countenances, or have experienced a mighty change in our hearts. This feeling is indescribable but it is real. Happy are those who have discovered within themselves His power to transform their lives, that comes from a kinship, a harmony, and an resilient connection with our Lord, Who is the Savior of the world.

March 11

"As many as are
not stiff necked and have
faith, have communion with
the Holy Spirit, which maketh
manifest unto the children
of men, according
to their faith."
(Jarom 1:4).

The
devil's
proposal
denied free
will by requiring
obedience based on
coercion. Today, those
who become entrenched in
sinful practices find it very hard
to break their bad habits, because
they have given up their agency in
order to acquire them. They find
themselves ensnared by Satan,
bound by his strong chains,
and feel the heavy cords
around their necks as
they are speedily
dragged down
to hell.

March 12

The
wicked are as the
"raging waves of the sea,
foaming out their own shame;
wandering stars, to whom is
reserved the blackness of
darkness forever."
(Jude 1:13).

It is not only in
the media, but also in our
common experience, that we are
assaulted by scribes and Pharisees
with golden tongues who beguile us
with worldly wisdom, politically correct
behavior, and with homogenized values.
They tempt us with subtle sophistry and
words like tolerance, equal opportunity,
and affirmative action. Ever so gently,
they nestle flaxen cords around our
necks. It all seems so reasonable, so
comfortable, so inclusive, and so
open-minded, that we scarcely
notice our surroundings, that
we are being maliciously
led down a terrifying
highway to hell.

March 13

"The man is become as one of us, to
know good and evil; and now, lest he put
forth his hand, and take also of the tree of
life, and eat, and live for ever. Therefore
the Lord God…drove out the man, and
he placed at the east of the garden of
Eden Cherubims, and a flaming
sword which turned every
way, to keep the way
of the tree of life."
(Genesis 3:22-24).

When
we reach the age of
accountability, we must be
born again. It cannot be a question
of our development, or our maturation,
but rather of our generation. One of the most
emotional and awe-inspiring events of mortality
is birth. It would be difficult to more dramatically
conceptualize in metaphor the miraculous process
of kindling the divine spark, of awakening our
potential, or of igniting the spirit that lies
dormant within the god in embryo,
than to say that we must be
born again in order to
experience eternal
life.

March 14

"This greater priesthood administereth the gospel" of Jesus Christ, "and holdeth the key of the mysteries of the kingdom, even the key of the knowledge of God." (D&C 84:19).

The Spirit speaks "of things as they really are, and of things as they really will be," which are manifest in plainness "for the salvation of our souls." (Jacob 4:13). In contrast is intellectual embroidery that is at times preferred to the whole ensemble of the gospel; the frills to the fabric, as it were. Only revelation provides us with absolute anchors that we so desperately need. If we give it a chance, we will find that there is more realism in the word of God than there could ever be in a secularism that is congenitally short sighted.

March 15

"And
immediately there
fell from his eyes as it had
been scales, and he received
sight forthwith, and arose,
and was baptized."
(Acts 9:18).

Joseph Smith said that
as we approach perfection,
our views become clearer and our
enjoyments are greater, until we reach
the point where we have overcome evil and
have lost our desire for sin. Those who have been
born again leave behind their former lives, and become
quickened to spiritual realities. They covenant never again
to return to their wicked ways. They change their names and
become "saints, a translation of a Greek word also rendered
'holy,' the fundamental idea being that of consecration or
separation for a sacred purpose. The word came to
mean 'free from blemish,' whether physical or
moral. In the New Testament, the saints
are all those who by baptism have
entered into the covenant."
(Bible Dictionary).

March 16

"Enlarge the
place of thy tent…and
strengthen thy stakes."
(Isaiah 54:2).

We need to begin right
now to think about making
room in our congregations for the
Children of the Covenant, whomever
they may be or wherever they may live, as
the gathering of Israel gains momentum. "For
Zion must increase in beauty, and in holiness.
Her borders must be enlarged. Her stakes must
be strengthened. Yea, verily I say unto you…..
arise and put on (your) beautiful garments."
(D&C 82:14). The Lord our God shall set up
the ensign of the church in the Last Days
"for the nations." (2 Nephi 21:12). As He
told Joseph Smith: "I have sent mine
everlasting covenant into the world
to be a light to the world, and to
be a standard for my people,
for the Gentiles to seek to
it; to be a messenger
before my face."
(D&C 45:9).

March 17

"But the very hairs
of your head are
all numbered."
(Mathew 10:30).

We are
all the legitimate
offspring of eternal beings,
and deeply rooted within each of
us are the seeds of greatness, for we
have been endowed with the potential to
completely develop the attributes of our Father.
We muster His power by recommitting ourselves
to our covenants with Him. We believe in, and fight
for, the most profound truths and highest standards.
We are set apart to accomplish these tasks because
ours is an eternally significant work that is carried
out in partnership with our Creator. We are set
apart by our convictions, by our enthusiasm,
by our righteousness, and by our faith. It
is our constant prayer that those who
are within the warm embrace of
our influence will be blessed,
and will enriched, because
of His magnificent work
that has been given
into no hands
except our
own.

March 18

"Look
on the fields,
for they are white,
already to harvest."
(John 4:35).

As late as one hundred and
fifty years after the organization of the
church, missionaries were actively proselyting
in fewer than half the nations of the earth. By 2016,
missionaries were present in roughly 162 countries in the
world. As of 2016, the gospel has not been introduced in 57
countries, among them Afghanistan, Algeria, Burma, China,
Cuba, Egypt, Greenland, Iraq, Kuwait, Libya, Monaco, Nepal,
North Korea, Sudan, United Arab Emirates, and the Vatican
City. One gets the idea. Between 1830 and 1970, The Book
of Mormon had been translated into 25 languages, but
in the next 11 years, there were an additional 25
language translations. Much work remains to
be done, but currently (2016) The Book
of Mormon has been translated in
its entirety into 94 languages,
with portions available
in an additional 20
languages.

March 19

"Stand therefore, having
your loins girt about with truth,
and having on the breastplate
of righteousness."
(Ephesians 6:14).

Putting on the whole
armor of God gives us unbridled
confidence as we obey every one of His
commandments, as well as when we cultivate
the desire to participate in every ordinance that is
necessary to attain eternal life. But a potential conflict
arises when there is a discrepancy between priesthood
authority and power. The one comes by the laying on of
hands, and the other thru righteousness. At times, when
those who hold the priesthood are asked to officiate in
the ordinances, they do so without the supporting
power of Christ. Their acts are validated only
because of their ordination and because of
the sustaining faith of those to whom
they minister. We can see why the
Savior would admonish us:
"Be ye clean that bear the
vessels of the Lord."
(3 Nephi 20:41).

March 20

"And I saw
the dead, small and
great, stand before God;
and the books were opened,
and another book was opened,
which is the book of life, and the
dead were judged out of those
things which were written
in the books, according
to their works."
(Revelation 20:12).

"The Book
of Life is the record of
our acts that has been written
in our own bodies; engraven on
our bones, sinews, and flesh. That is,
every thought, word, and deed has an
effect on the human body; all these
leave their marks which can be
read by Him who is eternal
as easily as the words of
a book can be read."
(Bruce McConkie).

March 21

"Who is my mother?
And who are my brethren?...
Whosoever shall do the will of my
Father which is in heaven, the
same is my brother, and
sister, and mother."
(Matthew 12:48-50).

It was President Ezra Taft Benson who once taught the young men of the priesthood: "No more sacred word exists in secular or holy writ than that of mother," which is the keystone of the gospel arch and central to the Plan of Salvation. Without mothers there would be no one to participate in the Plan. As no other people do, the Latter-day Saints recognize the responsibility of mortal parents to provide nurturing environments for the spirit children of our Heavenly Father. Spencer W. Kimball said: "Mothers have a sacred role. They are partners with God, Who has placed women at the very head waters of the human stream."

March 22

"I
beheld
this great
and abominable
church; and I saw
the devil, that he was
the founder of it."
(1 Nephi 13:6).

The
prophets bless
us with the eternal
truths of the gospel, in
plainness and simplicity, so
that all might understand. It is
the nature of the apostolic calling
to bear witness to all of the world of
the divinity of the Savior and to teach
the path to salvation and exaltation in
ways that are easily understood. Since
the Bible is today ambiguous, unclear,
and even contradictory, it must be the
result of errors of both omission and
commission that were introduced
by uninspired, untutored, and
even maliciously motivated
copyists over the course
of three millennia
and more.

March 23

"If thou
knewest the gift
of God, and who it is
that saith to thee, Give
me to drink, thou wouldest
have asked of him, and he
would have given thee
living water."
(John 4:10).

When the
Lord established
His church, it was
His purpose to provide
for each of His children, be
they humble or proud, rich or
poor, strong or weak, the chance
to associate with their equals in an
uplifting environment that would be
infused by an atmosphere that would
nurture a religious basis upon which
they could build relationships. It is
to the extent that we fail to seize
these heaven-sent opportunities
that we remain strangers and
foreigners with each other
and with God, starving
our souls and further
diminishing our
spirits.

March 24

"Though heaven
and earth pass (away), one
jot or one tittle shall in no
wise pass from the law,
till all be fulfilled."
(Matthew 5:18).

In the Last Days, one
of the signs of the times will be
that the gospel will be taught with a
manifestation of great power to all people.
One day, there will be no need to teach others
the first principles of the gospel because we will
all know the Lord. "Then the heathen that are left round
about you shall know that (it is) I the Lord (who has built)
the ruined places, and (has planted) that that was desolate."
(Ezekiel 36:36). The earth will be renewed and will receive a
paradisiacal glory. "For behold," declared the Lord thru
His prophet Isaiah, "I create new heavens and a new
earth: and the former shall not be remembered, nor
come to mind." (Isaiah 65:17). "For the Lord shall
comfort Zion; he will comfort all her waste
places, and he will make her wilderness
like Eden, and her desert like the
(secret) garden of the Lord."
(Isaiah 51:3).

March 25

"The
pillars of
heaven tremble
and are astonished
at his reproof."
(Job 26:11).

Jesus Christ
is the Architect of
the cosmos, including
the "Pillars of Creation,"
elephant trunks of interstellar
gas and dust in the Eagle Nebula,
some 6,500 - 7,000 light years from
Earth. In an 1857 sermon by London
pastor Charles Haddon Spurgeon titled
"The Condescension of Christ," Spurgeon
used the phrase to describe both the physical
world and the force that binds it all together,
stemming from the Divine. "Now wonder, ye
angels," Spurgeon wrote of the birth of Christ,
"the Infinite has become an infant; He, upon
whose shoulders the universe doth hang,
nurses at his mother's breast; He who
created all things, and bears up
the pillars of creation."

March 26

"But
his wife
looked back
from behind him,
and she became
a pillar of salt."
(Genesis 19:26).

It is
our faith that
sets us free from the
self-defeating behaviors of
confusion, doubt, ignorance, sin,
worry, and guilt, that can cause us to
become immobilized, and even paralyzed,
during our mortal experience. In a garden setting,
Adam and Eve were blessed with freedom to act, but we
can forfeit that birthright thru the adoption of bad habits. We
are detained by telestial traffic jams, confused by conceptual
cul-de-sacs, and detoured by doctrinal dilemmas of our
own making. If we follow the strait and narrow way,
we will find that path opening up onto the broad
boulevards of unlimited opportunity that lead
directly to the perfect law of liberty, and to
an expression of mind, body, and spirit
that unerringly guides us toward the
surety that is described in the
scriptures as the Rest of
the Lord.

March 27

"And now, my
son, I have somewhat
to say concerning the thing
which our fathers call a ball, or
director – or our fathers called
it Liahona, which is, being
interpreted, a compass."
(Alma 37:38).

The
powerful symbolism
that is found in the familiar
expression "Liahona" comes down
from the distant past and the forgotten
language of the fathers, and so it had to be
interpreted by Alma as "compass" for modern
day readers. (See Alma 37:38). That the Liahona is
an object lesson for us all, is made evident by Alma's
comment to his son "that these things are not without
a shadow, for as our fathers were slothful to give heed
to the compass they did not prosper; even so it is with
things which are spiritual." (Alma 37:43). As it was
for Alma and for Helaman, so it is for us. It is the
Word of Christ that becomes our Liahona, and
if we set our course by its bearings, we will
find that there can be no wind that blows
except it fills our sails to carry us ever
closer to a safe harbor and a quiet
anchorage in the comfortable
and familiar surroundings
of our home port that
is nothing short of
heaven.

March 28

"Yea, thus saith
the still small voice,
which whispereth through
and pierceth all things, and
often times it maketh my
bones to quake while it
maketh manifest."
(D&C 85:6).

We
are all in
desperate need
of inspiration, but it
may not come easily. In
fact, it is often preceded by
perspiration. Where there is no
student, there can be no revelation,
for "truth comes only to the prepared
mind." (Emerson). On one occasion, Joseph
Smith asked: "Does it remain for a people who
never had faith enough to call down one scrap of
revelation from heaven, and for all they have now
are indebted to the faith of another people who
lived hundreds and thousands of years before
them, does it remain for them to say how
much God has spoken and how much
he has not spoken?" (H.C. 11:17-18).

March 29

"The field
is the world."
(Matthew 13:38).

Because he
knew that Idumea's
image consultants would
confuse conventional wisdom
with the weightier matters of the
law in the tumultuous last days on
earth, Mormon cautioned: "Take heed,
that ye do not judge that which is evil to
be of God, or that which is good and of God
to be of the devil." (Moroni 7:14). In the vast
arena that is the world, there are no shades of
gray for those who have not only received the
Light of Christ, but also the greater power of
the Holy Ghost. For to them it is given "to
judge, that (they) may know good from
evil; and the way to judge is as plain,
that ye may know with a perfect
knowledge, as the daylight
is from the dark night."
(Moroni 7:15).

March 30

"Thou hast hid these
things from the wise and
prudent, and hast revealed
them instead unto babes."
(Matthew 11:25).

Who are these valiant
spirits, the poet asked, that seem
to be "coming down like gentle rain through
darkened skies, with glory trailing from their feet
as they go, and endless promise in their eyes? Who are
these young ones growing tall, growing strong, like silver
trees against the storm; who will not bend with the wind or
the change, but stand to fight the world alone? These are the
few, the warriors saved for Saturday, to come the last day of
the world. These are they, on Saturday. These are the strong,
the warriors rising in their might to win the battle raging in
the hearts of men, on Saturday. Strangers from a realm of
light, who have forgotten all; both the memory of their
former life, and the purpose of their call. So, they
must learn why they're here, and who they
really are." (Doug Stewart).

March 31

"I have prepared
a great endowment
and (a) blessing."
(D&C 105:12).

Our temple
endowment consists of
covenants of action between us
and our Father, including the bestowal by
ordinance of the spiritual and priesthood power
necessary to overcome the influences of the world, to
pass the sentinels who guard the way, and to part the veil,
that we might enter into the Rest of the Lord. We do not need
to fear in our hearts, when we are conscious of having lived up
to our covenants. When we are diligent in our obedience, our
agency enjoys its greatest expression. This is the power that
is unleashed in the House of The Lord. It is one of the
hardest things for the unconverted to understand
that some things just need to be believed, and
to be experienced, in order to be seen.

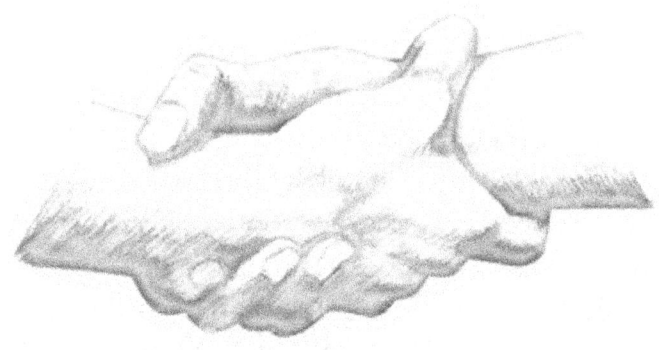

April 1

"And suddenly
there came a sound from
heaven as of a rushing mighty
wind, and it filled all the house
where they were sitting."
(Acts 2:2).

We
are all subject
to the immutable
laws of cause and effect.
As long as those who bear
the burden of sin find it within
themselves to focus their faith on the
Atonement of Christ, which is the only
mechanism that is capable of nullifying the
consequences of their poor choices, and if they
also muster the fortitude to do whatever needs to
be done to draw His power into their own lives, they
will uncover the gifts of the Spirit. All who have faith in
the ability of Christ to save them from their sins will have a
profound motivation to live in accordance with His will. They
will enjoy an eternal perspective because they see with the eye
of faith. They will not only believe in Christ, but they will also
believe Christ when He says that they can inherit celestial
glories. The striking manifestation of spiritual gifts will
provide dramatic validation to their persistent efforts
to conform their lives to His nature. They will raise
their voices to testify that they have experienced a
change in their hearts, and within themselves
have felt the urge to join with angels in the
praise of God, and to sing the song of
redeeming love. (See Alma 5:26).

April 2

"For, behold, the day
cometh, that shall burn as an oven;
and all the proud, yea, and all that do
wickedly, shall be stubble: and the day
that cometh shall burn them up,
saith the Lord of Hosts, that it
shall leave them neither
root nor branch."
(Malachi 4:1).

Jacob addressed
all those who gun their
engines in telestial traffic jams,
become hoarders of temporal trash,
and who have a fascination with trivial
pursuits: "Wo unto him...that wasteth the
days of his probation, for awful is his state!"
(2 Nephi 9:27). Particularly when individuals
groan "under darkness and under the bondage
of sin," they have no hope and their lives have
little meaning or stability. (D&C 84:49). They
cannot begin to comprehend that fame is a
vapor, and popularity is an accident, and
those who cheer you today may curse
you tomorrow; that, in the end, the
only thing that endures, the only
thing that you can really count
on, is your character. And
that is something upon
which you cannot
put a price.

April 3

"And righteousness
shall be the girdle of his
loins, and faithfulness the
girdle of his reins."
(Isaiah 11:5).

The Plan was
designed to fortify us
through our participation in
repetitive patterns of righteous
behavior. When we develop habits
that are consistent with the principles of
the Plan, we are protected from the influences of
the world that would otherwise leave us vulnerable
to the enticements of the devil. The terrible effect of sin on
those who have previously been taught the principles of the
gospel is that the guidance of the Spirit is withdrawn, and they
are left alone to grope in darkness. Guilt causes them to shrink
from church activity, and in the absence of the Spirit, sinners
can have no claim on blessings, prosperity, or preservation.
Tragically, those who feel uncomfortable when they are in
a close proximity to spiritual experiences, withdraw to
lifestyles devoid of such associations. Thus, begins a
downward spiral that can only gain momentum as
sinful practices that are more easily committed
become habitual. Seen too oft, familiar with
the face of sin, those who at first pitied
the disobedient, find themselves
enduring and then embracing
the darkness that aforetime
had seemed abhorrent
to them.

April 4

"And
the Lord
called his people
Zion, because they
were of one heart and
one mind, and dwelt in
righteousness; and there
was no poor among them."
(Moses 7:18).

It is
only with the
mentality of Zion
that we can find the
righteousness to break up
mountains, and the priesthood
power to "divide the seas, to dry up
waters, to turn them out of their course;
to put at defiance the armies of nations, to
divide the earth, to break every band, to stand
in the presence of God." (J.S.T. Genesis 14:30-31).
Zion grasps arrows in one talon and an olive branch
with the other. "I will cause the heavens to shake for
your good, and Satan shall tremble and Zion shall
rejoice upon the hills and flourish." (D&C 35:24).
The wicked shall be as Belshazzar of old, who
found himself in awkward circumstances;
so much so that his thoughts troubled
him, and he found "the joints of his
loins were loosed, and his knees
smote one against another."
(Daniel 5:6).

April 5

Over time,
Joseph Smith grew
increasingly confident
in God's promise to support
him" against all the fiery darts of
the adversary," and to be with him
"in every time of trouble."
(D&C 3:8).

Nephi clearly
taught that, in the Last
Days, Satan would once again
raise the spectre of rebellion, and he
would "rage in the hearts of men, and stir
them up to anger against that which is good."
(2 Nephi 28:20). As the process of the Restoration
unfolded, Satan fought a desperate battle to prevent
the receipt, translation, publication, and distribution
of The Book of Mormon. Having failed in his efforts,
he now attempts to substitute the sophistry of men
for the simplicity of the message. But that fraud is
all form and no substance, because it contributes
nothing to the welfare of Zion. Its driving force
seems to be a brazen craving for personal gain,
with a duplicitous message that is propelled
by a perceived power that is nothing more
substantive than the fleeting adoration
of an irrational world that, in its blind
fanaticism has completely lost sight
of its objectives. Its only option,
it appears, is to hysterically
redouble its efforts in
the absence of a
Plan.

April 6

They
"shall drink
of the wine of the
wrath of God, which
is poured out without
mixture, into the cup
of his indignation."
(Revelation 14:10).

Those
who have
become enslaved
by selfish indulgence to
the point that they "regard
not the work of the Lord, neither
consider the operation of his hands,"
must ultimately drink of the wine of the
wrath of the indignation of God. (2 Nephi
15:12). Without knowledge of heaven, they
are as those who are "famished, and their
multitude dried up with thirst. Therefore,
hell hath enlarged herself, and opened
her mouth without measure; and their
glory, and their multitude, and their
pomp, and he that rejoiceth, shall
descend into it (even as) God
that is holy (is) sanctified
in righteousness."
(2 Nephi 15:13-16).

April 7

"Labour
not for the meat
which perisheth, but for
that meat which endureth
unto everlasting life, which
the Son of man shall
give unto you."
(John 6:27).

In 1967, the
Boston Globe reported:
"Mormons can be a lot like
artichokes. At first encounter, you
either like them or you don't. But those
who have had unfavorable first impressions
often find that once the outer layers have been
peeled away, both Mormons and artichokes are
quite enjoyable. In fact, most people who take
the time to get to know Mormons become
their friends, and after a little objective
research regarding their beliefs, it is
revealed that, with the exception
of a few doctrinal differences,
those who call themselves
Latter-day Saints are just
like the rest of us, and
are very human
beings."

April 8

"And now also the axe is laid unto the root of the trees. Therefore every tree which bringeth not forth good fruit is hewn down and cast into the fire." (Matthew 3:10).

The ignorance of worldly wisdom is bad enough; however, a poor grasp of eternal principles lies at the root of apostasy from the truth. Even today, the church suffers from a shallow understanding by many members of even basic gospel doctrines. Consequently, the devil seizes upon their weaknesses. Satan knows who the Lord's servants are; each one is a marked man or woman. Therefore, they all require for a defense a solid foundation of doctrinal knowledge, an abiding testimony of every principle of the Plan of Salvation, as well as a witness of the Savior and Redeemer of the world.

April 9

"Thou shalt
break them with a
rod of iron. Thou shalt
dash them in pieces like
a potter's vessel."
(Psalms 2:9).

The
cold, logical,
and measured
rational thought
of secular humanism
that governs "our age is
retrospective, building on
the sepulchers of the fathers. It
writes biographies, histories, and
criticism. The foregoing generations
beheld God and nature face to face; we,
through their eyes. But why should we not
also enjoy an original relation to the universe?
Why should we not have a poetry and philosophy
of insight and not only of tradition, and a religion by
revelation to us, and not just the history of theirs?" (R.
W. Emerson). If we will recommit ourselves to study the
revealed word of God, we will find that Alma's promise
is true; that it will have a great tendency to lead us to do
what is right. In fact, it will exert a more powerful
effect upon us than the sword, or anything
else which could have wrought upon
us, to change our behavior.
(See Alma 31:5).

April 10

"He shall judge among the nations, and shall rebuke many people. And they shall beat their swords into plowshares, and their spears into pruning hooks. Nation shall not lift up sword against nation, neither shall they learn war any more."
(Isaiah 2:4).

We may not be able to do everything, but we surely can do something to stem the advancing tide that oozes from the cesspool of iniquity. First, we need to remember that it is better that we light a candle than curse the darkness. A thousand points of light, taken together, will cast a very long shadow. Abraham Lincoln soberly reminded us: "To sin by silence, when words should be spoken, makes cowards of men." As Isaiah wrote: "Lift up thy voice with strength."
(Isaiah 40:9).

April 11

The
covenant people
of the Lord "are built
upon the foundation of the
apostles and prophets, Jesus
Christ himself being the
chief corner stone."
(Ephesians 2:20).

There were counted
among the earliest Hebrews
a number "whose tired eyes could
see beyond the desert to those invisible
summits of the imagination where cool air
existed and where the one god, El Shaddai, he
of the mountain, existed. In later generations, El
Shaddai would reveal Himself as the only deity
worshipped by much of the world. But for now,
these people were sure of one thing. El Shaddai
personally determined the little band's destiny,
for of all the people available to him between
the Euphrates and the Nile, He had chosen
these Hebrews as his predilected people,
and they lived within his embrace, and
enjoyed a security that was foreign to
others," that they could never hope
to completely understand or to
adequately explain to their
unconverted neighbors.
(James Michener).

April 12

"The wages of sin is death, but the gift of God is eternal life through Jesus Christ." (Romans 6:23).

The decay of our physical bodies is necessary to satisfy the requirements of the merciful Plan of our Father. But our spiritual death is far more serious, because it happens when we die "as to things pertaining unto righteousness." (Alma 12:16). The first spiritual death occurs when we commit sin after the age of accountability. We can be spiritually born again, however, through the sanctifying influence of the Holy Ghost, after repentance and baptism by immersion. But there is also a second spiritual death, which is eternal separation from God's presence that transpires after we have passed from mortality to immortality without having beforehand received all of the ordinances of the priesthood, and when we thereafter deny the Lord a second time, by willingly declining the ordinances of the priesthood that have been performed on our behalf in the House of the Lord.

April 13

"Come now, and let us reason together, saith the Lord. Though your sins be as scarlet, they shall be as white as snow; though they be red like crimson, they shall be as wool."
(Isaiah 1:18).

The character and nobility of those of us who are fortunate enough to dwell in the neighborhood of Zion is the inevitable result of a spiritual transformation as we live the Celestial Law of the Lord. The power of the Atonement allows us to "come out of the world and leave the loneliness and the estrangement of a fallen creation" and then to "enter the realm of divine experience. We forsake the orphanage of spiritual alienation, and are received into the family and household of Jesus Christ." We leave the ranks of the nameless and take up residence with the blameless. In time, we become joint-heirs of all that our Father has.
(Lael Woodbury).

April 14

"There is laid
up for me a crown of
righteousness, which the
Lord, the righteous judge,
shall give me at that day;
and not to me only, but
unto all them also that
love his appearing."
(2 Timothy 4:8).

It is
without malice
aforethought that the
righteous receive the image of
the Lord in their countenances. Their
faces naturally reflect the Light of Christ.
Because of the mighty change in their hearts,
they are new creatures in Christ, created to reach
their potential in both the image and likeness of
God their Father. Their testimonies become the
foundation for a sustained saving faith that
gives them confidence to stand tall before
the pleasing bar of God, to bask in the
embrace of His holy presence, to be
weighed in the balances, and by
His good grace to receive His
approbation, as well as
their inheritance in
His kingdom.

April 15

"The
new heavens
and the new earth,
which I will make, shall
remain before me."
(Isaiah 66:22).

Those who have entered the fold at the
waters of baptism take their responsibility to
share the gospel very seriously. They follow the
example of St. Patrick, whose character "converted
the Irish with the undoubting confidence of his belief, as
well as the passionate persistence of his work. He ordained
priests, built churches, established monasteries and nunneries,
and left strong spiritual garrisons to guard his conquests at every
turn. He gathered about him men and women of courage and
devotion who endured every privation to spread the good
news that man was redeemed. He did not convert all
Ireland; some pockets of paganism and its poetry
survived, and leave traces to this day. But
when he died in 461 A.D., it could be
said of him, as no other, that one
man had converted a nation."
(Will Durant).

April 16

"The Lord God is a sun
and shield. The Lord will give
grace and glory. No good thing
will he withhold from them
that walk uprightly."
(Psalms 84:11).

Our firm and unshakable
testimony of the great Plan of Deliverance
from Death will forever govern ignorance, and
will thereby become the catalyst of our purposeful
action. As we seek to gain an understanding of both
the temporal and eternal worlds, we will develop the
power to exercise true moral agency. Comprehension
will come "line upon line and precept upon precept."
(D&C 98:11-12). It will stay with us, and it will rise
with us in the resurrection, affording us tangible
advantages in the eternities. Our life beyond
the veil offers the tantalizing promise of an
exponential expansion of our knowledge
that will be accompanied by an
awakening re-acquaintance
with heaven itself.

April 17

"Think not that I am
come to send peace on
earth. I came not to send
peace, but a sword."
(Matthew 10:34).

Tom Paine wrote
of the tumultuous Last
Days in which we are privileged
to live, that these are truly "the times
that try men's souls. The summer soldier
and the sunshine patriot will in this crisis shrink
from the service of his (fellow-citizens); but he that
stands it now, deserves the love and thanks of (every
man. Adversity), like hell, is not easily conquered, yet
we have this consolation with us, that the harder the
conflict, the more glorious is the triumph. What we
obtain too cheap, we esteem too lightly. Dearness
only gives everything its value. Heaven knows
how to put a proper price on its goods, and
it would be strange, indeed, if so celestial
an article as (our understanding of the
Plan) should not be highly rated."
("Common Sense").

April 18

"The inhabitants of the earth have been made drunk with the wine of her fornication." (Revelation 17:2).

Pointedly and specifically to all those whose weak character has enslaved them in drunkenness and selfish indulgence, ancient prophets have spoken a powerful message. "Wo unto them that rise up early in the morning, that they may follow strong drink, that continue until night, and wine inflame them!" (2 Nephi 15:11). Those who senses have been dulled by excess of any kind can be blinded to the pattern of progress that is before their eyes. "They regard not the work of the Lord, neither consider the operation of his hands." (2 Nephi 15:12). They are captive because of physical addictions and are bound with a stupor of thought. Because they have become so telestially traumatized, they have no comprehension of God. "Their honorable men are famished, and their multitude (has been) dried up with thirst." (2 Nephi 15:13).

April 19

"Blessed are the
meek, for they shall
inherit the earth."
(Matthew 5:5).

In all of the ages
of time, the meek have reflected
poise under provocation, have been slow to
anger, and have been particularly sensitive to the
needs of others. They are empathetic and humble.
They are less concerned with telestial trinkets and
are more focused on celestial sureties. The meek
are selfless, and they have no secret agenda to
follow. They are repulsed by sin and rejoice
in the truth, are drawn toward the light,
and are continually open to that which
is good. Meekness may be one of the
greatest of all the qualities of God
Himself, Who is the possessor
of all spiritual gifts. Without
it, we are nothing, because
our progress toward our
Divine Center cannot
establish traction or
sustain forward
momentum.

April 20

"Lay up for yourselves treasures in heaven, where neither moth nor rust doth corrupt, and where thieves do not break through nor steal."
(Matthew 6:20).

Our conceit notwithstanding, we should never expect to be so self-reliant, self-indulgent, arrogant, or wealthy that we could ever think that it would be possible to purchase the gifts of the Spirit with the profane treasures of the earth. Perhaps this is why in their efforts to obtain the sacred records, the Lord allowed the sons of Lehi to be stripped of all their gold, silver, and precious things by Laban. The task that He had set before them was to be accomplished in His own way, and by the power of His mighty arm, which is great in the sight of the faithful, but which has a terrible effect upon the wicked. Alma, who must have been familiar with the records of his fathers, asked the age old question: How could we ever "dispute the power of God?"
(Mosiah 27:15).

April 21

"Forgive us
our debts, as we
forgive our debtors."
(Matthew 6:12).

Just
as soon as we
have learned this life
lesson, the better off we will
be. It is that we can do absolutely
nothing that puts God in our debt. The
more obedient we are, the more He blesses
us, and the more indebted to Him we become.
Finally, even as we view with the clear lens of
faith our "nothingness" before God, our hope
is perfected "through the Atonement of Christ
and the power of his resurrection." We have a
perfect assurance that we will be "raised up
unto life eternal, and this because of (our)
faith in him according to the promise."
(Moroni 7:41). This assurance is the
inevitable result of well-founded
faith, when we are "meek
and lowly of heart."
(Moroni 7:43).

April 22

"Wilt thou not place a stumbling block in my way; but that thou wouldst clear my way before me."
(2 Nephi 4:33).

The trials that we face today are really not any more sophisticated than those of our forbearers. Noah warned his people about a coming deluge. Our prophets warn us about the rising tide of pornography that is inundating the world. Moses chronicled the bondage of Israel in Egypt. Today, we are at risk of the temporal bondage of financial indebtedness. Elijah rebuked those who worshipped Baal. Our own prophets warn us of the spiritual servitude that follows the worship of the popular idols of the day. Anciently, prophets described the depravations of Gandianton bands. The Doctrine & Covenants warns against the evil designs of conspiring men and women in the Last Days.
(See D&C 89:4).

April 23

"I
have fed
you with milk,
and not with meat.
For hitherto ye were
not able to bear it."
(1 Corinthians 3:2).

Eager novitiates
who have only recently
been baptized as members of
the church need to be taught the
first principles and basic doctrines of
the gospel, in order to strengthen their
faith. The question that should be on the
minds of those to whom a stewardship
responsibility of teaching falls, is: Are
we giving new members skim milk,
2% milk, or milk whose shelf life
has passed the expiration date?
Or, are we instead providing
them with the whole, fresh,
nutritionally fortified and
organically certified
milk that they
need?

April 24

"Let us
cleanse ourselves
from all filthiness of the
flesh and spirit, perfecting
holiness in the fear of God."
(2 Corinthians 7:1).

With only a few
clicks of a mouse, or with just
one or two keystrokes, even those
who have few computer skills can be
transported directly "into enemy territory
without having to first pass through passport
control." (Neal A. Maxwell). Knowledge can be
a dangerous thing if it is not accompanied by the
Spirit of God. "O that cunning plan of the evil one!
O the vainness, and the frailties, and the foolishness
of men! When they are learned they think they are
wise, and they hearken not unto the counsel of
God, for they set it aside, supposing they
know of themselves, wherefore, their
wisdom is foolishness and it
profiteth them not."
(2 Nephi 9:29).

April 25

"Save
me, O my
God, for thou
hast smitten all
mine enemies upon
the cheek bone. Thou
hast broken the teeth
of the ungodly."
(Psalms 2:7).

In spite of our best efforts to
gain a foothold and establish traction
on the telestial turf that we call our home,
it sometimes can be frustrating to us that we
still seem to be losing ground. "Now, here, you
see," the Red Queen patiently explained to Alice
in Wonderland, "it takes all the running you can
do, to keep in the same place. If you want to get
somewhere else, you must run at least twice as
fast as that!" (Lewis Carroll). Let us never
forget that one plus the Lord always
constitutes a majority. With His
help, we may run and not
be weary, and walk
and not faint.

April 26

"Let him
write her a bill
of divorcement."
(Deuteronomy 24:1).

We become successful
partners in our marriages as
we struggle to gain self-mastery by
overcoming adversity, and conquering
the cankered nature that predisposes us to
be disobedient to true principles. As we move
from dependency to independency, and then to
the more mature state of inter-dependency, our
marriage covenant helps us to focus our efforts
to become as God is. If marriage were viewed
as a probationary state, as a time of testing,
or of putting to the proof our envisioned
standard of behaviors, and if all were
done within the bounds the Lord
has set, its participants would
be less likely to bail out at
the first indication of
disenchantment
or tedium.

April 27

"Thou
preparest a
table before me
in the presence of
mine enemies; thou
anointest my head
with oil; my cup
runneth over."
(Psalm 23:5).

"Our
thanksgiving
to Heavenly Father
includes (gratitude) for
his tutoring of us to aid our
acquisition of needed attributes
and experiences while we are in
mortality." (Neal Maxwell). We
trust Him as the designer of
our coat of many colors,
whose fabric has been
masterfully tailored
to meet each and
every need.

April 28

"And, behold, the
veil of the temple was
rent in twain from the
top to the bottom."
(Matthew 27:51).

I am drawn to the Mountain of the
Lord's House, there to be washed that I
might become clean from the contamination
of the world, anointed with the oil of gladness,
clothed in the garment of God's protection, and
endowed at the hands of the priesthood, I will
claim the blessings of heaven as I strive to do
all that I must to mature into the full stature
of my spirit. I will be sealed to my loved
ones, and with them ascend to Zion,
where I will be reunited with my
extended family and enjoy the
familiar setting of my
eternal home.

April 29

"The spirit of man is
the candle of the Lord."
(Proverbs 20:27).

"I believe the state we enter
after death will be beautiful with
colour, music, and speech of flowers and
faces I love. Without this faith, there would be
little meaning in my life. I should be a mere pillar
of darkness in the dark. Observers in the full enjoyment
of their bodily senses pity me, but it is because they do not
see the golden chamber in my life where I dwell delighted.
For as dark as my path may seem to them, I carry a magic
light in my heart. Faith, the spiritual strong searchlight,
illuminates the way, and although sinister doubts may
lurk in the shadows, I walk unafraid towards the
Enchanted Wood where the foliage is always
green, where joy abides, nightingales nest
and sing, and where life and death are
one in the presence of the Lord."
(Helen Keller, "Midstream").

April 30

"Come
unto me,
all ye that
labour and are
heavy laden, and
I will give you rest."
(Matthew 11:28).

The prophet Ezra
revealed something about his
character, when he acknowledged:
"At the evening sacrifice I arose up from
my heaviness, and rent my garment and my
mantle. I fell upon my knees, and spread out
my hands unto the Lord my God, and said I
am ashamed and blush to lift up my face to
thee, for our iniquities are increased over
our head, and our trespass is grown up
unto the heavens." (Ezra 9:5-6). "Then
Ezra rose up from before the house
of God…and he did eat no bread,
nor drink water." (Ezra 10:6).

May 1

"The Lord hath made bare his holy arm in the eyes of all the nations; and all the ends of the earth shall see the salvation of our God." (Isaiah 52:10).

Anciently, as well as in our day, God has laid bare His arm and shown His power, in order to lead His chosen people Israel out of captivity, to bring her out of obscurity and darkness, and to gather her to the lands of her inheritance, that she might know that the Lord is her Redeemer. What the devil and his followers do not understand is that real power and violence are mutually exclusive. When one is present, the other must be absent. The arm of the Lord is our source of strength and support, in contrast to the arm of flesh that is unstable and volatile, and is subject to the types of erratic outbursts that are directed at no one in particular, that are spectacularly ineffective, and are frustratingly self-defeating.

May 2

"Why should I give
way to temptations, that
the evil one have place in my
heart to destroy my peace
and afflict my soul?"
(2 Nephi 4:27).

Temptation is
a powerful narcotic,
which makes Lucifer the
quintessential drug dealer. He
was "a son of the morning," whose
influence over Heavenly Father's children
was truly impressive. His name meant "Light
Bearer," and so he was. In the Great Council, he
offered to redeem all mankind. But even then, he
lacked the faith necessary to allow agency to rule.
He concocted an inoperable counterfeit plan that
would have denied its participants the powers
to exercise free will in order to create positive
change. Because of his passionate, and yet
misguided, promotion of this spurious
proposal, the scriptures refer to him
as Satan, the father of lies, and
as a liar from the beginning,
meaning from before the
foundation of the
world.

May 3

"Ye are the salt of the
earth. But if the salt have lost
his savour, wherewith shall it be
salted? It is thenceforth good
for nothing, but to be cast
out, and to be trodden
under foot of men."
(Matthew 5:13).

We
are reinvigorated
to share the gospel with
our own neighbors when we
read the account in the Book of Alma,
wherein Ammon metaphorically described
a harvest, that he might illustrate how thousands
and thousands of wicked Lamanites had been gathered
through the missionary efforts of his brethren, known as
the Sons of Mosiah. "Behold, the field was ripe," he said, "and
blessed are ye, for ye did thrust in the sickle, and did reap with
your might, yea, all the day long did ye labor; and behold the
number of your sheaves!" (Alma 26:5). His party had come
up out of the Land of Zarahemla into the highlands of
Nephi to bring a message of love to the Lamanites.
In its absence, their kinsmen "would still have
been racked with hatred (against their
brethren the Nephites), and they
would also have (remained)
strangers to God."
(Alma 26:9).

May 4

"There
arose a mist
of darkness; yea,
even an exceedingly
great mist of darkness,
insomuch that they who
had commenced (on) the
path did lose their way,
that they wandered
off and were lost."
(1 Nephi 8:23).

Following
the betrayal, trial, and
crucifixion of the Lord, the word
was spat out: "Christian!" But the Saints
continued to live their lives as He had taught
them, and the world, illuminated by the inspired
ministry of His authorized servants, was suddenly
aflame with faith. When the light finally dimmed,
dark mists swirled about, sowing wickedness at
every turn. And so it came to pass, that in the
crucible of that refiner's fire, the humble
followers of the Good Shepherd were
asked, once again, to wear their
title with dignity.

May 5

"But with
righteousness
shall he judge the poor,
and reprove with equity for
the meek of the earth. And he
shall smite the earth with the
rod of his mouth, and with
the breath of his lips shall
he slay the wicked."
(Isaiah 11:4).

In the
scriptures, the
"rod" can be a symbol
of the active engagement of
priesthood power. The Lord has
revealed His battle plan for the Last
Days, when His missionary army will
engage the worldly, whose corruptible
ideology will be vanquished. They may
be reborn spiritually in the face of the
bombardment of love unfeigned, the
onslaught of priesthood principles,
and by the crushing clout that is
characteristic of the powerful
covenants that the penitent
have always embraced
when their faith has
convicted them of
their sins.

May 6

"All
grain is
ordained for
the use of man
and of beasts to be
the staff of life."
(D&C 89:14).

"They that
wait upon the Lord
shall renew their strength,
they shall mount up with wings as
eagles, they shall run, and not be weary,
and they shall walk, and not faint." (Isaiah 40:31). Long ago, it was recognized that there exists a relationship between obedience to the commandments and physical well-being; that when we consciously and deliberately adopt lifestyles that lead to poor physical health,
"wisdom cannot reveal itself, culture
cannot become manifest, strength
cannot fight, wealth becomes
useless, and intelligence
cannot be applied."
(Heraclitus).

May 7

I
would that
ye "would have
repented long ago
in sackcloth and ashes."
(Matthew 11:21).

With our fasting, the
spiritual and temporal sides
of our nature slowly harmonize,
until they reach a state of balance and
equilibrium. Physical desires are tempered by
a spiritual awareness that strengthen our resolve
to discipline our carnal nature. We transcend the forces
that pull us one way or the other, and enter a metaphysical
state of euphoria. Virtue garnishes our thoughts as the doctrine
of the priesthood distills upon our souls as the dews from heaven,
because our confidence begins to wax strong in the presence of
God. As this process unfolds, the Holy Ghost becomes our
constant companion, our scepter an unchanging scepter
of righteousness and truth, and our dominion a God
centered and focused province of protection. With
these conditions governing our lives, all that
is good will begin to freely flow unto us
in an unending stream for now
and for all of eternity.
(See D&C 121:45-46).

May 8

"And
also cometh
the testimony of the
voice of thunderings, and
the voice of lightnings, and
the voice of tempests, and the
voice of the waves of the sea,
heaving themselves beyond
their bounds."
(D&C 88:90).

Since
time immemorial,
it has been the vision
and the quest of the righteous
that they might obtain the Rest of
the Lord. That spiritually stable state of
equilibrium is a steady beacon of hope to
the faithful, standing in sharp contrast to the
telestial trauma inflicted by wars and rumors of
wars, that are so commonplace today. Peace of mind
and spirit is born of a settled conviction of the truth in
our hearts. Today, even in the midst of adversity, and as
the order of society crumbles around us, we enter God's
Rest by coming to an understanding of the truths of the
gospel, and then by living our lives in harmony with
celestial principles. His peace is "the peace born of
the righteous life, the peace that lifts the soul,
that day by day brings us closer to the
home of Eternal Peace, that is the
dwelling place of our Father."
(J. Reuben Clark, Jr.).

May 9

"These
are they whose
bodies are celestial, whose
glory is that of the sun, even the
glory of God, the highest of all,
whose glory the sun of the
firmament is written of
as being typical."
(D&C 76:70).

A casual, or
an indifferent, unattached
recognition of the Lord Jesus Christ
will never qualify squatters on the world
stage to receive an inheritance of celestial glory.
These Christians of convenience lack the fire in the
belly that is characterized by discipleship. Honorable
people whose faith in the Savior is uncommitted will
inherit only terrestrial glory as their eternal reward,
because they "received not the gospel, neither the
testimony of Jesus, neither the prophets, neither
the everlasting covenant. Last of all, these are
the everlasting covenant. Last of all, these are
all they who will not be gathered with
the saints, to be caught up unto the
church of the Firstborn, and
received into the cloud."
(D&C 76:101-102).

May 10

"Other
sheep I have,
which are not of
this fold. Them also
I must bring, and they
shall hear my voice, and
there shall be one fold,
and one shepherd."
(John 10:16).

"In the
Hellenistic age,
Jews were dispersed
over the entire Greek world.
As early as 140 B.C.E., the author
of the Sibylline Oracles testified that
the whole land and seas were full of Jews.
A contemporary of Herod said it would have
been hard to find a place in the world where there
were no Jews. And Josephus added: 'There are no
people in the world among whom part of our
brethren is not to be found.' Philo spoke
of the wide expansion of the Jews
throughout the world, and of
Jerusalem as the center of
the scattered nation."
(Abba Eban).

May 11

"In the beginning
was the Word, and the
Word was with God,
and the Word
was God."
(John 1:1).

If
we are ever
going to inherit our
exaltation and enjoy eternal
life with our Father in Heaven, we
must do more than just acknowledge
that Jesus Christ is Lord. The critical point
of conversion, beyond which lie the circling flames
of fire in the Celestial Kingdom of God, rests in making
a conscious decision to accept not only the Savior, but also
His gospel. A simple yet uncommitted recognition of Jesus
does not qualify us to live with Him forever. Christians of
convenience lack the fire that the demands of discipleship
require. Only those who have passionately embraced
the gospel with its ordinances and covenants, and
who are subsequently mentored by the Master,
may walk the path that leads to the highest
degree of glory within the Celestial
Kingdom of God, where they
will live forever in His
holy presence.

May 12

"Though I
walk through
the valley of the
shadow of death,
I will fear no evil,
for thou art with me.
Thy rod and thy staff
they comfort me."
(Psalms 23:4).

If
I lose
sight of
the way that
lies before me, I
have the Liahona to
guide me unerringly.
As a compass, it allows
me to focus on eternity.
Without it, I know that
my progress would
falter, leaving me
to wander in the
desert wastes
of Babylon,
alone and
afraid.

May 13

"I will
put the law
in their inward
parts, and write it
in their hearts, and
will be their God, and
they shall be my people."
(Jeremiah 31:33).

It was the
psalmist who wrote
from the perspective of a
broken heart and a contrite spirit:
"But as for me...my clothing was sackcloth.
I humbled my soul with fasting." (Psalms 35:13).
When the law is written upon our hearts, and we feel
God's forgiveness, we must seize at that very moment the
opportunity to forgive others, invoking spiritual power to
bless our efforts, precisely because it is so contrary to our
nature to do so. The opportunity to forgive should never
be wasted, because it can awaken within our hearts a
spiritual sensitivity that is somehow greater than
ourselves. Brigham Young told the Saints that
"he who takes offense when no offense was
intended is a fool, and he who takes
offense when it was intended is
usually a fool."

May 14

"Let us therefore fear,
lest, a promise being left us of
entering into (God's) rest any
of you should seem to
come short of it."
(Hebrews 4:1).

As the
poor disciples of
Christ who eschew the
trappings of a tangible telestial
tailoring, we are allowed to enter into
His Rest only after we have been carried
away by a personal vision of our potential;
that is to say, if we smite the destroyer with the
power of the word, and live life enthusiastically.
As with a divine fire, we are filled with the Spirit,
and are caught up unto eternal life to enjoy perfect
knowledge of the divinity of the work of the Lord.
We rest from all fear, doubt, apprehension, danger,
religious turmoil, and from the vagaries of men.
The peace that we know as God's Rest is our
recompense for undistracted obedience to
the celestial principles that, taken as
a whole, are God's own majestic
clockwork calibrated with
its orientation on the
eternities.

May 15

"For the
Son of Man is
Lord, even of the
Sabbath day."
(Matthew 12:8).

In the
modern world,
we think it would be
insane to put to death those
who violate the Sabbath Day; yet
we die spiritually when we estrange
ourselves from God's influence, because
we have put a halt to our eternal progression.
Brigham Young felt that the dominion God gave
to us was designed to test us, and to enable us to
show just how we would act if entrusted with
His power. He has created a special time of
the week as a work release program that
allows us to show Him how we might
behave when left on our own, after
having received instructions that
pointedly teach us what we
ought to be doing on
this, His holy
day.

May 16

"The people
of the church began
to wax proud, because of
their exceeding riches, and
their fine silks, and their
fine-twined linen."
(Alma 4:6).

Satan,
is a dedicated
deceiver who knows
all the tricks of the trade.
He advocates evil by making
drinking and smoking look enticing,
and by rationalizing cheating, lying, and
stealing. He plays mind games to encourage
drug use, and he clothes the latest fashions in fine
twined linens. Immorality and swearing are woven
into popular music and hit movies. He minimizes
the seriousness of sin by telling us: "Everyone's
doing it." "It doesn't hurt anyone else." "Just
once won't hurt." "I can always repent."
"It's not a big deal." And even, to
our amazement: "The devil
made me do it."

May 17

"We
shall not sleep,
but we shall all be
changed, in a moment, in
the twinkling of an eye."
(1 Corinthians 15:51-52).

"I
will
praise thee
with my whole
heart; before the
gods will I sing praise
unto thee." (Psalms 138:1).
In that millennial day, we will
live in a state akin to translation.
Our bodies will no longer be subject to
disease or death as we know it, although
we will be changed in the twinkling of
an eye. Isaiah prophesied that during
the thousand years of peace, "there
shall be no more thence an infant
of days, for the child shall die
an hundred years old."
(Isaiah 65:20).

May 18

"And the
Lord appeared unto
Abram, and said, Unto
thy seed will I give this
land" of promise.
(Genesis 12:7).

Not only the
Land of Canaan, but
also sundry other locations
throughout the world may be
legitimately characterized as Lands
of Promise. Many groups over the years
left Jerusalem in search of these lands. The
Dead Sea Covenanters who lived at Qumran
near the shores of the Salt Sea have become the
most conspicuous in our day. But there certainly
were many other righteous families who, during
the millennia, were similarly guided by the Spirit
amid deteriorating conditions in Israel to flee into
the wilderness, where the Lord could love them
freely, and where His anger would be turned
away. (See Hosea 14:4). They would be free
to pledge to each other their lives, their
fortunes, and their sacred honor. The
Lord would be as a dew, and Israel
would grow as the lily, and cast
forth his roots as Lebanon.
(See Hosea 14:5).

May 19

"And the Lord
shall guide thee continually,
and satisfy thy soul in drought,
and make fat thy bones; and thou
shalt be like a watered garden,
and like a spring of water,
whose waters fail not."
(Isaiah 58:11).

Those who have feasted
upon the scriptures, and have
really sunk their teeth into them and
savored them; who have prayed for help
in digesting them, and have then sought to
receive a witness that what they've devoured is
true, know what spiritual hunger is. It is when the
powers of heaven and earth amplify each other and
lift us up on harmonic waves. When we experience
moments like this, it is as if someone has given us
"gospel glasses" to wear. Everything seems to
resonate more clearly, and we feel as if we
have suddenly been granted the eternal
perspective that we have for so long
been searching, that we might
satisfy our celestial
cravings.

May 20

"His
garments must
be purified until
they are cleansed
from all stain."
(Alma 5:21).

Each
morning,
as the shafts
of golden sunlight
resonate at the dawn of a
new day, and I rub the sleep
from my eyes, I will be resolute,
as I persist in my firm determination
to conduct my affairs that I might always
be honest, true, chaste, benevolent, virtuous,
and do good to others. As my faith increases, so
will my capacity to see God's influence over every
aspect of my life. I will learn to recognize and accept
the suffering that is a part of life, and will strive to see
adversity as a necessary and beneficial component of my
experience. In times of trial, I will remember the Savior,
Who descended beneath all things, and Who set the
example for me. I will be drawn to the light. It will
become part of my nature to relate comfortably
with that which is virtuous, lovely, of good
report, or praiseworthy. Anything that
charges my soul, creates a nurturing
atmosphere, or encourages
improvement, is worthy
of my pursuit.

May 21

"They
have escaped
the pollutions of
the world through
the knowledge of the
Lord and Saviour
Jesus Christ."
(2 Peter 2:20).

The
terrifying torrent of
filthy water that was beheld
by Lehi in vision represented "an
awful gulf which separated the wicked
from the tree of life, and also from the saints
of God." (1 Nephi 12:16). The Plan of Salvation
requires that there always exist a barrier between
the spirits of the righteous and the unrighteous,
as both await the resurrection. That barrier is
nothing more than the justice of God "and
the brightness thereof (is) like unto the
brightness of a flaming fire, which
ascendeth up unto" heaven
"forever and ever."
(1 Nephi 15:30).

May 22

"He leadeth me beside
the still waters."
(Psalms 23:2).

As we bow
with our knees and
confess with our tongues,
we acknowledge His leadership
and we emulate His example. He sets
the course, and we follow the guidelines
He has established. He gives commandments,
and we yield to His will. He requires obedience, and
we accept the rewards for following through, as well as
the consequences for willful neglect of our responsibilities.
We consented to the risks attendant to mortality, because we
believed in the Plan, and we knew He would never leave us.
When our foundation is firmly grounded on the bedrock of
gospel principles so that we feel His presence, we can be
certain of our ultimate success, because we know that
it was foreordained in heaven to be so, long before
the world was. At the end of the day, only by
following with exactness every principle of
the Plan will we find the elusive solution
to our salvation. Although the worldly
cannot seem to comprehend God's
explanation of exaltation, it is
the only one that resonates
within us to make sense
of the mysteries
of life.

May 23

"And whosoever
shall not receive you, nor
hear your words, when ye
depart out of that house
or city, shake off the
dust of your feet."
(Matthew 10:14).

If those who
have been taught the
gospel reject the Spirit's
invitation to sit and sup with
the Saints, perhaps it is because
their stiff neck has prevented them
from looking up to Heavenly Father for
guidance, over to men of God for counsel,
around to seek answers to life's most profound
questions, or down in an attitude of humility. It
is the challenge of those who have found the joy
of the gospel to soften the telestial tendencies of
their friends and neighbors, and find the keys
that will open their hearts, that they might
be softened and become as pliable clay
in the creative hands of the
Master Potter.

May 24

"The
good seed
are the children
of the kingdom."
(Matthew 13:38).

Seeds that have
been lovingly sown and
then carefully nurtured in fertile
gospel soil have an excellent chance
of blossoming into strong, healthy plants
with deep roots. These seeds are the covenants
that we make with God. They derive their healing
powers from their association with the firm foundation
of His holy character. In our church experience, we are like
the good seeds that have matured into a forest of trees that are
secure in numbers. When the winds of adversity blow hard,
we are unified and strengthened by our solidarity. But if
we try to stand alone, no matter how great the girth
of our trunks, no matter how securely planted we
think our roots are, we risk toppling over. We
become as solitary 'widow-maker' trees
that have been carelessly left in the
forest after its clearing.

May 25

"Wash me,
and I shall be
whiter than snow."
(Psalms 51:7).

In language
that is both refreshing
and unique, Mormon recorded that
as the resurrected Lord ministered among
His Nephite disciples, "he did smile upon them,
and behold they were as white as the countenance and
also the garments of Jesus; and behold the whiteness thereof
did exceed all the whiteness, yea, even there could be nothing
upon earth so white as the whiteness thereof." (3 Nephi 19:25).
They had been sanctified in the redeeming blood of Christ,
and by His grace had been saved. They now enjoyed the
sweet companionship of the Second Comforter and
their faces reflected His light. In our own day,
the Lord has re-affirmed that if our eyes
be single to His glory, our whole
bodies shall be filled with
light, and there shall be
no darkness in us.
(See D&C 88:67).

May 26

"As one
whom his mother
comforteth, so will
I comfort you."
(Isaiah 66:13).

When
young Joan of Arc
stood before the stake,
and was offered her freedom
by denying what she believed, she
instead declared: "I know this. Every man
gives his life for what he believes. Every woman
gives her life for what she believes. Sometimes people
believe in little or nothing, and so they give their lives
for little or nothing. One life is all we have, and we
live it as we believe in living it, and then it is
gone. But to surrender what you are, and
to live without belief, is more terrible
than dying. It is even more
terrible than dying
young."

May 27

"Prove me
now herewith, saith
the Lord of hosts, if I will
not open you the windows of
heaven, and pour you out a
blessing, that there shall
not be room enough
to receive it."
(Malachi 3:10).

Nothing
that is short of
the very best that
we can provide is good
enough for the Lord, and so
our tithe is no more than a token.
We consecrate that which we are, for
God requires more than an uncommitted
gesture of faith. Our offering before his throne
is found within ourselves; it is in our hearts. It
is not just a tenth part, but is our complete
devotion to the will of our Father, Who
is our Benefactor and the Provider
of, not what we ever hope to
have, but what we ever
hope to be.

May 28

"O
death, where is
thy sting? O grave,
where is thy victory?"
(1 Corinthians 15:55).

The two
most important
days of our lives, that
should be commemorated
with celebration and joy, are the
day we were born, and the day we
find out why. After we have come to
understand our purpose, our lives will
never again be the same, up until the day
we die, when we really discover why we
lived. When we begin to comprehend the
grammar of the gospel, we see, as Neal A.
Maxwell observed, that "death is a mere
comma, and not an exclamation point!"
The light has not been extinguished;
rather the lamp has been put out
because the dawn has arrived.
Death is nothing more than
an artificial horizon that
limits our sight.

May 29

"The day of
the Lord so cometh
as a thief in the night."
(1 Thessalonians 5:2).

Our Lord and Savior
Jesus Christ told the Prophet
Joseph Smith that He would reveal to
all of His followers the unmistakable signs
of His Second Coming. He said: "Be not troubled,
for, when all these things shall come to pass, ye may
know that the promises which have been made unto you
shall be fulfilled." (D&C 45:34-35). Prior to that event, it will
once again be as it was just before the birth of the Savior, when
great signs were given in Zarahemla "to the intent that there
should be no cause for unbelief," and also "to the intent
that whosoever" would muster the faith to "believe
might be saved." (Helaman 14:18-19). Finally, at
His Second Coming, He will reveal Himself
"from heaven with power and great glory"
to those who have faithfully waited for
the dawn of the millennial day, and
He will dwell in righteousness
with them on the earth for
a thousand years.
(D&C 29:11).

May 30

"Every city or house
divided against itself
shall not stand."
(Matthew 12:25).

Those in
Zion see with
wide-eyed wonder.
Babylon squints at every
sunburst that heralds a spiritual
awakening, and would rather put on
designer sunglasses than adjust its eyes to
the increased illumination of the light of truth.
Zion abases the wealthy in order to exalt the poor.
Babylon emphasizes the treasures of the earth, worships
the almighty dollar, trades in counterfeit currency, destroys
initiative through a misguided sense of entitlement, allows
ambition to replace righteous desire, and suppresses
upward mobility and progress by maintaining
the status-quo and subjugating the interests
of those who are no less deserving, but
who are, through no fault of their
own, in much less fortunate
circumstances.

May 31

"Out of the throne
proceeded lightnings,
and thundering,
and voices."
(Revelation 4:5).

The
inhabitants
of the earth "shall
see my face and know
that I am," declared the Lord.
(D&C 93:1). "The veil shall be rent and
you shall see me, not with the carnal neither
natural mind, but with the spiritual." (D&C 67:10).
Our Father gives us this clarity "to the intent that there
should be no cause for unbelief," and also "to the intent
that whosoever will believe might be saved, and that
whosoever will not believe, a righteous judgment
might come upon them; and also if they are
condemned they bring upon themselves
their own condemnation."
(Helaman 14:28-29).

June 1

"He was a
murderer from
the beginning, and
abode not in the truth,
because there is no truth in
him. When he speaketh a lie,
he speaketh of his own,
for he is a liar, and
the father of it."
(John 8:44).

The
mental
and emotional
abuse of psychological
warfare were characteristic of
Lucifer's insurgency. It was out-
and-out rebellion, a struggle for our
minds, as conflicting ideologies grated
against each other. The misery caused was
profound, with souls not a few cut off from
God's presence. So many bright lights were
dimmed in the struggle! With weeping, and
wailing, and with gnashing of teeth, those
who fell forfeit both their birthright and
the promise of increase, as their final
expression of free will destroyed
both their desire and their
ability to comply with
the equitable laws
of heaven.

June 2

"He hath
power given unto him
from the Father to redeem
them from their sins because of
repentance; therefore he hath sent
his angels to declare the tidings of the
conditions of repentance, which bringeth
unto (them) the power of the Redeemer,
unto the salvation of their souls."
(Helaman 5:11).

If we
violate God's
laws, our conscience
encourages us to recognize
the error of our ways. It allows
us to experience feelings of remorse
for having committed the sin, to right
the wrong if it is within our power to do
so, to refrain from repeating it, to repent of
our errant behavior, to receive forgiveness,
and then to move on with our lives. It is in
the Atonement of Christ, and it alone, that
our stumbling blocks can be miraculously
transformed into stepping-stones. Only
then will mortality, with its potholes
and pitfalls, become the growth
experience that the heavens
designed it to be.

June 3

"Arouse
the faculties of your
souls. Shake yourselves,
that ye may awake from
the slumber of death."
(Jacob 3:11).

Every society on the face
of the earth has always paid a heavy
price for its lack of vision, as it has closed
its collective mind and heart to an expansion
by the Spirit. The Dark Ages remain the worst-case
scenario, but in many respects we are once again living
in that stifling era. Every time a culture loses its spiritual
equilibrium, it seems to re-adjust its values in an expedient
realignment with worldly coordinates. Today, worship of gods
of wood and stone is justified as multiculturalism. Perversion is
embraced and legitimized as an alternative lifestyle. The poor are
exploited under the guise of programs sponsored by government.
Unborn children are torn from mother's wombs, and the collective
conscience is assuaged by calling it pro-choice. The gross abuse
of power is justified as the means to an end. Every obscenity
pollutes the media, but new-speak characterizes it as the
freedom of speech. The target has been moved so often
that self-congratulatory pundits believe that they are
scoring bulls-eyes when they are really far from the
mark. The prophet Isaiah saw our day, when he
warned Israel: "Wo unto them that call evil
good, and good evil; that put darkness
for light, and light for darkness; that
put bitter for sweet sweet, and
sweet for bitter."
(Isaiah 5:20).

June 4

"By fire
and by his
sword will the
Lord plead with
all flesh, and the
slain of the Lord
shall be many."
(Isaiah 66:16).

Elder Mark E. Petersen
declared that in the midst of the
trials and tribulations that will become
even more commonplace in the Last Days,
"God will send fire from heaven if necessary to
destroy our enemies while we carry forward our
work." The Master of the Universe would never
permit Satan or his lieutenants to thwart His
purposes, no matter how hard they might
try. As a matter of fact, those who have
"perverted the right ways of the Lord,
yea, that great and abominable
church, shall tumble to the
dust, and great shall
be the fall of it."
(1 Nephi 22:14).

June 5

"The Lord
hath poured
out upon you the
spirit of deep sleep,
and hath closed your
eyes. The prophets and
your rulers, the seers
hath he covered."
(Isaiah 29:10).

The mind-numbing tedium
and monotony of the unrelenting
stretch of years between 400 and 1000 A.D.
has been characterized as the Dark Ages, a time
that was stark in every dimension. Intellectual life had
vanished from Europe. Even Charlemagne, the first Holy
Roman Emperor and the greatest of all medieval rulers,
was illiterate. In all those static centuries, absolutely
nothing of real consequence had either improved
or declined. With the sole exception of the
introduction of waterwheels in the 800^s,
there were no inventions of note. A
creative vacuum existed, where
everything remained as it
had been for as long
as anyone could
remember.

June 6

"But of the fruit
of the tree which is in
the midst of the garden,
God hath said, Ye shall
not eat of it, neither
shall ye touch it,
lest ye die."
(Genesis 3:3).

Our Heavenly Father
always honors agency, which
has been recognized as the guiding
principle of heaven. It entails risk, but
it is the only way for us to progress. Rather
than enslaving us in good habits, He repeatedly
gives us the opportunity to recommit ourselves to
true and eternal doctrines and to covenants of action.
Agency allows each of us to enjoy all of the privileges
of church membership, empowers us to remain active,
and is the principle that sanctions our commitment to
baptismal promises, all of which are essential if we
are to nourish our spiritual wellbeing. Only with
agency, can we gyroscopically maintain our
spiritual equilibrium and hope to manage
the mercurial fluidity of a world whose
only constant seems to be its harsh
and unrelenting proclivity to
continually reinvent
itself.

June 7

"Lift up
your eyes to the
heavens and look upon the
earth beneath. For the heavens
shall vanish away like smoke, and
the earth shall wax old like a garment,
and they that dwell therein shall die in
like manner. But my salvation shall
be forever, and my righteousness
shall not be abolished."
(Isaiah 1:6).

At the dawning of the
millennial day, the confidence
of the people in government will be
restored, for it will be righteous. The word
of the Lord will flow, from not one, but from
two capitals. "For out of Zion shall go forth the
law, and the word of the Lord from Jerusalem."
(Isaiah 2:3). There will be no disease or death.
When people have lived to an old age, they
will not die in the classical sense, but will
be changed in the twinkling of an eye,
from a mortal state to immortality,
in a process that is described
as translation.

June 8

"Beware of false prophets, which come to you in sheep's clothing, but inwardly they are ravening wolves."
(Matthew 7:15).

Our Lord and Savior warned that in the Last Days "many false prophets shall rise, and shall deceive many." (Matthew 24:11). He did not say that there would be no prophets, but only that there would be great confusion because of those imitators whose message is often accompanied by the kind of gaudy paraphernalia that attracts the curious, but that demands little commitment. Just as as moths are drawn to fire, the unwary flirt with death in a deadly duet with the flickering flame of deception and lies.

June 9

"An evil
and adulterous
generation seeketh
after a sign."
(Matthew 12:39).

The real
problems that most
of us face are that we receive
too little revelation, and also that
we look for it in all the wrong places. The
prophets' repeated warnings against dalliances
with magicians, sorcerers, witches, familiar spirits,
astrologers, and exorcists are as relevant today as they
were long ago. We must avoid participating in divinations,
enchantments, and other activities that solicit the intervention
of evil spirits. Isaiah mocked those who relied on such, when
he said: "Thou art wearied in the multitude of thy counsels.
Let now the astrologers, the stargazers, the monthly
prognosticators, stand up, and save thee from
these things that shall come upon thee.
Behold, they shall be as stubble;
the fire shall burn them."
(Isaiah 47:13-14).

June 10

"And they who keep
their first estate shall be added
upon...and they who keep their
second estate shall have glory
added upon their heads
for ever and ever."
(Abraham 3:26).

The Lord revealed to His
prophet Moses: "I made the world, and
all men before they were in the flesh." (Moses
6:51). To Jeremiah, He explained: "Before I formed
thee in the belly I knew thee; and before thou camest
forth out of the womb I sanctified thee, and I ordained
thee a prophet unto the nations." (Jeremiah 1:4-5). Moses
was asked to "remember the days of old...when the most
High divided to the nations their inheritance. When he
separated the sons of Adam, he set the bounds of
the people according to the number of the
children of Israel." (Deuteronomy
32:7-8). The scriptures clearly
testify us that we lived
before we were
born.

June 11

"He was wounded for our transgressions; he was bruised for our iniquities. The chastisement of our peace was upon him, and with his stripes we are healed." (Isaiah 53:5).

It might be of some comfort to know that "if we were to close the doors upon sorrow, we might very well be excluding our greatest friends and benefactors. Suffering can make saints of us as we learn patience and self-mastery. If we looked at mortality as the whole of existence, then pain, sorrow, failure, and short life would be calamity. But if we look upon life as an eternal thing stretching far into the pre-mortal past and on into the eternal future, then all happenings may be put in proper perspective." (Spencer W. Kimball).

June 12

"For
this people's
heart is waxed gross,
and their ears are dull of
hearing, and their eyes
they have closed."
(Matthew 13:15).

Our certain,
and unwavering
comprehension of the
truth is made possible by
the irreproachable influence
wrought by the third member
of the Godhead, even the Holy
Ghost. Knowledge expedites the
application of moral agency that is
our properly channeled free will. It
provides us with power to hammer
out our salvation with both fear and
trembling before the Lord. Gaining
wisdom is critical to the successful
implementation of the Plan. Thus,
it is another of the spiritual gifts
that has been providentially
provided by the source of
all wisdom, Who is our
Father in Heaven.

June 13

"The
wolf also
shall dwell with
the lamb, and the
leopard shall lie down
with the kid, and the calf
and the young lion and the
fatling together; and a little
child shall lead them."
(Isaiah 11:6).

In the
Millennium,
those who remain
on the earth will not be
focused on a competition for
scarce resources. The scriptural
descriptions of millennial conditions
paint a portrait where righteousness
prevails; where "the earth is full of
the knowledge of the Lord, as
the waters cover the sea."
(2 Nephi 21:9).

June 14

"And they had power given unto them, insomuch that they could not be confined in dungeons."
(Alma 8:31).

"We who lived in the concentration camps can still remember those who walked through the huts comforting others, giving away their last piece of bread. They may have been few in number, but they offer sufficient proof that everything can be taken away from us but the one thing that is the last of the human freedoms, and that is to choose what our attitude will be," said Victor Frankel. We do this no matter how hard our circumstances may seem. We keep our own counsel, are our own guides, and determine that we will follow our own path, always firm in the faith that our steps will safely guide us to the peace and rest that are the sanctuary of the Lord.

June 15

"Above all," grasp "the
shield of faith, wherewith
ye shall be able to quench all
the fiery darts of the wicked."
(Ephesians 6:15).

Far too frequently and
always dishearteningly, it seems to
be our fatal inclination that when we fall
into the habit of neglecting to quickly repent of
our sins, we begin to feel uncomfortable when we are
in proximity to spiritual experiences, and we withdraw to
lifestyles that are devoid of such associations. Thus begins a
downward spiral that gains momentum as we become more
comfortable with our sinful behavior. "Thus saith the Lord
concerning all those who know my power, and have been
made partakers thereof, and suffered themselves through
the power of the devil to be overcome, and to deny the
truth and defy my power. They are they who suffer
spiritual death," or life without light and truth.
(D&C 76:31-32). This explains why, all
too often, "the man that doeth this,
the same cometh out in open
rebellion against God."
(Mosiah 2:37).

June 16

"Cease to speak evil
one of another."
(D&C 136:23).

When
we participate
in gossip, our focus
is on mindless chatter
and speaking without real
purpose. It is damaging, because
it voraciously feeds on vanity, rumor,
hearsay, and innuendo. If it is left unchecked,
it may build into a self-perpetuating chain reaction
leading to a whole series of unfortunate, yet inevitable,
consequences. In its many forms, gossip has one common
characteristic. Words so loosely spoken cannot be gathered
up later on. Like feathers left on the doorstep of those with
whom one has engaged in idle conversation, they will
have drifted to the four winds, and they cannot be
recalled. Words so carelessly scattered about
suggest that the mouth has been put in
motion before the brain has been
brought on-line.

June 17

"I send you forth as
sheep in the midst of
wolves. Be ye therefore
wise as serpents, and
harmless as doves."
(Matthew 10:16).

Over and over again,
those who have committed
to a serious study of the scriptures
are enjoined therein to put things in their
proper perspective; that they should not seek to
obtain riches, but wisdom, and that in order to have a
working understanding of spiritual things, they must have
discernment, which is guidance from the Holy Ghost. Those
who inquire with sincerity are taught by the Spirit, and the
confirmation of their faith is a manifestation of the special
gift of the Holy Ghost. One of the Lord's purposes is
to shepherd the covenant faithful by the power of
the Spirit from the waters of baptism, along
the strait and narrow path to the other
ordinances of the priesthood that
are necessary for them to
obtain eternal life.

June 18

"Hear ye this, O
house of Jacob, which are
called by the name of Israel,
and are come forth out of the
waters of Judah, which swear
by the name of the Lord,
and make mention of
the God of Israel."
(Isaiah 48:1).

God's elegant
solution for dealing
with the revolting filthiness of
our sins is to wash them away both
figuratively and literally in the healing
waters of baptism. The Manual of Discipline
from the Serek Scroll at Qumran reads: "His sin
is forgiven him and in the humility of his soul he
is for all the laws of God. His flesh is cleansed
shining bright in the waters of purification,
even in the waters of baptism, and he
shall be given a new name in due
time to walk perfectly in all
the ways of God."

June 19

"For I
know this, that
after my departing
shall grievous wolves
enter in among you, not
sparing the flock."
(Acts 20:29).

"The
ravening wolves
are amongst us from
our own membership, and
they, more than any others,
are in sheep's clothing, because
they wear the habiliments of the
priesthood. We should be careful
of them," said J. Reuben Clark Jr.
Ezra Taft Benson agreed: "There
are some in our midst who are
not so much concerned about
taking the gospel into the
world, as they are about
bringing worldliness
into the gospel."

June 20

"Behold,
I lay in Zion
for a foundation
a stone, a tried stone,
a precious corner stone,
a sure foundation."
(Isaiah 28:16).

We all need
to ask ourselves
these questions: What
do we want from life? Why do
we want it? How can we obtain it?
What are our short-term and long-term
goals? What are our temporal and spiritual
goals? How can we harmonize the two? We can
begin now to develop a foundation that is built
upon the principles of the Plan, that clearly
articulates a personal mission statement
that gives our lives definition and our
decisions meaning, and imbues
every action with a tangible
sense of positive
purpose.

June 21

"It shall
come to pass in
the last days, that the
mountain of the Lord's
house shall be established
in the top of the mountains,
and shall be exalted above
the hills, and all nations
shall flow unto it."
(Isaiah 2:2).

"Although
The Church of Jesus
Christ of Latter-day Saints
has earned a prominent part in
the great drama of the Last Days,
it is not the only force, nor the only
means, that the Lord has employed
in order to bring to pass the things
of which His prophets, in ancient
times, have testified."
(B.H. Roberts).

June 22

"He that troubleth
his own house shall
inherit the wind."
(Proverbs 11:29).

There
is a great
responsibility on
the part of children to
be obedient, so that they
may, in turn, teach their own
little ones in an unbroken pattern.
When parents have children in Zion, or
in any of her stakes which are organized,
and then fail to help them to understand the
doctrines of the kingdom, "the sin be upon the
heads of the parents. And their children shall be
baptized for the remission of their sins when
eight years old, and receive the laying on
of the hands. And they shall also teach
their children to pray, and to walk
uprightly before the Lord."
(D&C 68:25-28).

June 23

"I and my
Father are one."
(John 10:30).

The
awe-inspiring
redwoods of the Pacific
coast are among the largest of
living things, and take our breath
away. The tallest known tree reaches
a height of 368 feet, weighs hundreds of
tons, and is well over 2,000 years old. While
most other trees of nearly equivalent size have
deep roots to support their great weight, the root
system of the redwood is very shallow. The key to
its survival is the intertwining of the roots of one
tree with those of several of its neighbors. These
giants of the forest live in groves; they cannot
stand alone. Interdependence is critical to
the stability and longevity of each tree.
Just so, in the church, our hearts
are knit together in unity and
in love, one to another.
(See Mosiah 18:21).

June 24

"Bring my soul out of prison, that I may praise thy name."
(Psalms 142:7).

In the spirit world, the paradise of God is the abode of the righteous. The unrepentant go instead to the spirit prison of the unjust to await their day of redemption. That time will come if they accept the gospel of Jesus Christ and when necessary priesthood ordinances have been vicariously performed for them. Those in the spirit prison who reject the gospel, and thereby deny salvation through the power of the Atonement of Jesus Christ, will have to satisfy Justice by paying for their sins themselves. They will not be redeemed from the Fall until they have personally "paid the uttermost farthing."
(Matthew 5:26).

June 25

"These are
wells without water,
clouds that are carried
with a tempest, to whom
the mist of darkness is
reserved for ever."
(2 Peter 2:17).

"Little
people, like you
and me, if our prayers are
sometimes granted beyond all
hope and probability, had better
not draw hasty conclusions to our
own advantage. If we were stronger,
we might be less tenderly treated. If
we were braver, we might be sent,
with far less help, to defend far
more desperate posts in the
last great battle."
(C.S. Lewis).

June 26

"If ye will obey my voice indeed, and keep my covenant, then ye shall be a peculiar treasure unto me above all people." (Exodus 19:5).

In his second inaugural address to a youthful nation, Thomas Jefferson declared: "I shall need the favour of the One in whose hands we are, who led our forefathers, as he did Israel of old, from their native land, and planted them in a country flowing with the necessaries and comforts of life."

June 27

"The
race is not to
the swift, nor the
battle to the strong."
(Ecclesiastes 9:11).

"Dear
God, so far
today, I've done all
right. I haven't gossiped.
I haven't lost my temper. I
haven't lied or cheated others.
I haven't been greedy, grumpy,
nasty, selfish, or overindulgent,
and I'm very thankful for that,
as well. But, in a few minutes,
Lord, I'm going to get out of
bed, and from then on, I'm
probably going to need
a lot more help."
(Anonymous).

June 28

"The wilderness and the solitary place shall be glad for them, and the desert shall rejoice, and blossom as the rose." (Isaiah 35:1).

"Without faith we are free to do what we like, and that can be a pleasant feeling at first, because there are no questions of conscience and no constraints except those of custom, convention and law, and these are flexible enough for most purposes. It is only later that the terror comes. We are free, but only in the chaos of an unexplained and unexplainable world. We are free in a desert from which there is no retreat but inexorably inward toward the hollow core of ourselves." (Morris West). As Jarom exhorted in the 4th verse of his brief record: "Have faith, (and enjoy a) communion with the Holy Spirit."

June 29

"He
restoreth my soul. He
leadeth me in the paths
of righteousness for
his name's sake."
(Psalms 23:3).

The power to convey the meaning
of gospel principles to others is a gift of the
Spirit. It must reside in both the one who delivers
the word and the one who is receiving it. This is the
magic of gospel instruction. It is a foolproof method
for illuminating the good news, because it cannot be
mishandled or misrepresented. Without the Spirit,
we are as "sounding brass or a tinkling cymbal."
(1 Corinthians 13:1), As the Savior warned: "If
ye receive not the Spirit, ye shall not teach."
(D&C 42:14). This responsibility is so
great, that it is no wonder that we
are admonished: "Be ye clean
that bear the vessels of the
Lord." (Isaiah 52:11).

June 30

"I will make them
of the synagogue of Satan,
which say they are Jews, and
are not, but do lie. Behold,
I will make them to come
and worship before thy
feet, and to know that
I have loved thee."
(Revelation 3:9).

Who shall
declare himself for
the Lord, when taunted
by Spiritual Babylon? Or
who shall hold fast to the
rod of iron when the
mists of darkness
swirl about
him?

July 1

"Be ye not unequally
yoked together with unbelievers,
for what fellowship hath righteousness with
unrighteousness? And what communion
hath light with darkness?"
(2 Corinthians 6:14).

To
perform in
their roles to the
successful conclusion
of God's Trilogy (Where
did I come from? Why am
I here? and Where am I going?),
the disciples of Christ cannot have
the luxury during the production of
the Second Act to sample the pleasures
of Spiritual Babylon, to walk "in (its) own
way, after the image of (its) own god, whose
image is in the likeness of the world, and whose
substance is that of an idol." (D&C 1:16). Only if the
drama is played out within the parameters of the Plan,
according to the dialogue established by the principles
of the gospel that are expressed in its doctrines, can
anticipated blessings of Zion freely flow. There is no
other way. "Life is all a stage," wrote Shakespeare,
but only the script written by God, Who is our
Dialogue Coach, will bring out the best in
those who participate in the production.
We need to trust Him and in His His
approach, which may have been
the source of inspiration for
the most accomplished of
the method actors of
our day.

July 2

"He will lift up an ensign to the nation from far, and will hiss unto them from the end of the earth; and, behold, they shall come with speed, swiftly." (Isaiah 5:26).

The Lord will raise His voice, and thru electronic media, the summons will come from afar. The pure in heart will respond to that call, and will hasten to Zion with such alacrity that before they have had time to become tired, they will have arrived at their destination. "None shall slumber nor sleep; neither shall the girdle of their loins be loosed, nor the latchet of their shoes be broken." (Isaiah 5:27). During their travels, they will require neither rest nor a change of clothing. Isaiah further described the great commotion made by the iron wheels of railroad cars, and the sparking and flashing of the rails that run beneath horses' hooves. (See Isaiah 5:29).

July 3

"And the
Lord God formed
man of the dust of the
ground, and breathed into
his nostrils the breath of
life, and man became
a living soul."
(Genesis 2:7).

The element are indefatigable in their
obedience to their Creator, and even the
agency of sentient beings such as ourselves
is completely powerless to alter the progress
or influence the outcome of any or the least of
His directives. It is when we recognize our utter
dependence upon Him that it dawns upon us that
we are even less than the dust of the earth, which
thing we had never before supposed. There is
nothing we could do to put Him in our debt.
Just as it should be, our dependence upon
our Heavenly Father for our support is
total. It is complete in the sense that
He is the provider of all our needs.
In Him, we live and move and
have our being, as certain
poets have said; for we
are His offspring.
(See Acts 17:28).

July 4

"I have
covered thee in the
shadow of mine hand, that I
may plant the heavens, and
lay the foundations of the
earth, and say unto Zion,
Thou art my people."
(Isaiah 51:16).

At the
end of the day,
how we view life with
all of its inequities, comes
down to our simple, yet basic
decision to either complain about
everything that is wrong, or express
gratitude for everything that is right.
Whereas chronic complainers attract
negative energy, let us instead attract
the positive energy of the good news
that is the gospel, that it might be an
influence that is as authoritative as
the rolling stone that has been cut
out of a mountain, and that can
be channeled thru priesthood
power into a force for good
that will change for the
better the world in
which we live.

July 5

"To as
many as (have)
received me, gave I
power to become my
sons; and even so will I
give unto as many as will
receive me, (the) power
to become my sons."
(D&C 39:4).

In
nothing
that is short
of a transcendent
action of fidelity and
trust, God transfers His
power to mankind with no
purpose other than to bless us
as completely as is possible. The
only limitation to this magnificent
equation is the extent to which we
will permit Him to grant us grace.
In the end, it is we who will have
finally established the terms and
conditions for working out our
own salvation with fear and
trembling before He Who
is the Lord of lords,
and the King of
kings.

July 6

"It came to pass
that the burdens which
were laid upon Alma and
his brethren were made light;
yea, the Lord did strengthen them
that they could bear up their burdens
with ease, and they did submit" themselves "cheerfully and with patience to
…the will of the Lord" their God.
(Mosiah 24:15).

Each of
us owes our
life, right down
to the very core of our
existence, to a spiritual credit
that has been graciously extended
to us by our Heavenly Father. "One day
the account will be closed, and a settlement
demanded. However casually we may view it
now, when that day comes and the foreclosure
is imminent, we will look about in a restless
agony for someone, anyone, to help us. But
by eternal law, mercy cannot be extended
save there be one who is both willing
and able to assume our debt, pay
the price, and arrange the terms
of our redemption." (Boyd K.
Packer). We need look no
further than to our Lord
and Savior, Who is the
Redeemer of the
world.

July 7

"In that day,
shall the deaf hear the
words of the book, and the
eyes of the blind shall see
out of obscurity, and
out of darkness."
(Isaiah 29:18).

"Faith is things
which are hoped for and not
seen; wherefore, dispute not because
ye see not, for ye receive no witness until after
the trial of your faith." (Ether 12:6). It is important to
remember that in matters of faith, we, and not the Lord,
are on trial. Out of the sum of our experiences comes the
trial of our faith. At the Bar of Justice, which is eminently
fair, the evidence will be presented to an unbiased and
impartial Judge. Executing the provisions of the Plan,
He will allow our previous acceptance or rejection of
our faith-based experiences, measured against our
subsequent actions, to be the determining factor
that is related to the reward or the punishment
for which we have qualified. Ultimately, we
cannot escape the consequences that are
related to our behavior. It will be with
a profound sense of finality that
we must accept them, be
they good or bad.

July 8

"The word of
God is quick, and
powerful, and sharper
than any two edged sword,
piercing even to the dividing
asunder of soul and spirit, and
of the joints and marrow, and
is a discerner of the thoughts
and intents of the heart."
(Hebrews 4:12).

The
unalterable
demands of the
word of God necessitate
periodic withdrawals from
our spiritual savings accounts.
Our prior preparation requires us
to make dependable and consistent
faith-based deposits in anticipation of
these unavoidable runs on the bank. We
never permit ourselves to write checks
that cannot be cashed. We will always
live to be worthy of the cornucopia of
comfort and cushion of confidence
that are consistently created by a
courageous criterion of conduct
that eshews cowardice in
matters that pertain
to faith.

July 9

"He
that is
not with
me is against
me, and he that
gathereth not with
me scattereth abroad."
(Matthew 12:30).

The prominent
feature that is a paralyzing
phenomenon of the Last Days is that
our society is characterized by an unparalleled
polarization of principles that is accelerating at an
alarming rate. On the one hand, is the kingdom of God,
while on the other, is a moral and ethical depravity that is
nothing less than the cesspool of Satan, whose dominion is
typified as a corrupt or idolatrous community. There are,
after all, "save two churches only; the one is the church
of the Lamb of God, and the other is the church of
the devil, wherefore, whoso belongeth not to the
church of the Lamb of God belongeth to th
great church, which is the mother of
abominations; and she is the
whore of all the earth."
(1 Nephi 14:10).

July 10

"And Moses
made a serpent of brass,
and put it upon a pole, and it
came to pass, that if a serpent
had bitten any man, when
he beheld the serpent
of brass, he lived."
(Numbers 21:9).

The
scriptures teach
us that the way that
has been illuminated by
the principles of the gospel
should not be difficult to follow.
For the Israelites in the Wilderness
of Sinai, it was only necessary to look
to the Brazen Serpent, the staff of Moses
that typified Christ, in order to be saved.
"And as many as should look upon that
serpent should live, even so as many as
should look upon the Son of God, with
faith, having a contrite spirit, might
live, even unto that life which is
eternal." (Helaman 8:13-16).

July 11

"The Holy Ghost shall be thy constant companion, and thy scepter an unchanging scepter of righteousness." (D&C 121:46).

In our twenty-first century technological society, there could have been unleashed a joyous celebration and continuation of the Age of Enlightenment, but instead we are witnessing a conceptual free-for-all, with few rules, regulations, or restrictions to temper either moral or ethical depravity. The better angels of our nature respond to righteousness, because the positive energy of foundation principles is immune to the capricious character quirks of those who've compromised their standards in a capitulation to the telestial trauma of secular humanism. Those of weak will cannot deny their noble birthright for very long before it begins to strangle their spontaneity as rapidly evolving children of God. Obedience to our covenants, on the other hand, can bless our lives with a vitality that quickens our spirits in ways that nothing else can. The gospel is a living, breathing entity that is nourished by active involvement with its disciples, who are very much like you!

July 12

"For
the wisdom
of their wise and
learned shall perish,
and the understanding of
their prudent shall be hid."
(2 Nephi 27:27).

When we
naively exercise
prudence, we become
adept in following the most
politic and profitable course, but
our practicality can also lead us to be
circumspect, or cautious. In contrast, if we
approach life's questions with an attitude of
prayerful investigation, the qualities of worldly
wisdom and erudition will lose their value. If we
ever try to hide our counsel from the Lord, we will
find that our private purpose has only diminished
the potency of our inquiry. Only after the façade
of our artificial veneers has been stripped away,
can our spirits become prominently vulnerable
to the undeniable whisperings, the urgent
promptings, and the unmistakable
calls to action that come from
the Holy Ghost.

July 13

"If ye
continue in my
word, then are ye my
disciples indeed, and ye
shall know the truth,
and the truth shall
make you free."
(John 8:31-32).

The
gospel
of Jesus Christ
is the perfect law
of liberty, setting us free
to make intelligent choices,
free to receive the blessings of
priesthood, free to serve others
more meaningfully, and free to
enjoy unrestrained opportunity
for improvement, as we commit
ourselves to the observance of
proven principles. With the
gift of the freedom to act
independently, we are
free to follow a path
of progress, or a
path leading
to ruin.

July 14

"I saw
also the Lord
sitting upon a throne,
high and lifted up, and his
train filled the temple. Above
it stood the seraphims."
(Isaiah 6:1-2).

The Hebrew word
seraph means "burning," and
so the scriptures speak of "bright,
shining seraphs," and describe signs of
the coming of the Lord as "blood and fire,
and vapors of smoke." (D&C 45:41 & 109:79).
Metaphors of fire and smoke are used to depict
the glory of celestial realms. In the language of
Joseph Smith: "God Almighty Himself dwells
in eternal fire. Flesh and blood cannot go
there, for all corruption is devoured by
that fire. God is a consuming fire."
Perhaps one day, the rest of us
will come to understand just
how it is that immortality
dwells in everlasting
burnings.

July 15

"Whosoever heareth
these saying of mine, and
doeth them, I will like him unto
a wise man, which built his
house upon a rock."
(Matthew 7:24).

It
is an honor
and a privilege, in
fact, it is our destiny, to
conduct our affairs in such a
way that they are pleasing to God,
that will invite Him to accompany us
on life's journey as our faithful companion.
He is the bedrock of our salvation, as well as
the foundation upon which we build. In Him, we
have a sure footing that permits us to shake at the very
appearance of sin without jeopardizing the integrity
of our carefully coordinated components. Because
of Him, we are fitly framed, and the edifice of
our character reflects solid construction
that is of an enduring quality, and
that is a faithful representation
of exactly where we have
carefully positioned
our priorities.

July 16

"Wo unto you, scribes and
Pharisees, hypocrites! For ye
are like unto whited sepulchers,
which indeed appear beautiful
outward, but are within full
of dead men's bones, and
of all uncleanness."
(Matthew 27:23).

When
we are obsessed
with a blind obedience
and are overzealous in our
outward observances, we are as
hypocrites, pretending to be pious,
when, in fact, we are only professors
of religion. All too often, we creep into
nameless graves, while now and then,
as Phillips Brooks suggested, "one
or two of us forget ourselves
into immortality."

July 17

"Wherefore, the law was our
schoolmaster to bring us unto
Christ, that we might be
justified by faith."
(Galatians 3:24).

The outward observances
of ancient Israel were dictated
by the Torah, and were as phylacteries
that were reminders to keep the law. In our
day, real justification comes only through saving
faith in the principles and ordinances of the gospel.
However, there are always two distinctly different ways
that lie before each of us. "One leading to an ever lower
and lower plane, where are heard the cries of despair
and the curses of the poor, where manhood shrivels
and possessions wear down the possessor; and
the other leading to the highlands of the
morning where are heard the glad
shouts of humanity, and where
honest effort is rewarded
with immortality."
(John P. Altgeld).

July 18

"Your lamb shall
be without blemish."
(Exodus 12:5).

The Great
and Eternal Plan of
Deliverance from Death
has also been called the Plan of
Redemption, Mercy, and Happiness,
because it makes possible the resurrection
of otherwise imperfect souls to heavenly glory
and endless joy. These "great and eternal purposes
were prepared from the foundation of the world."
(Alma 42:26). "To the Son is given the power of
the resurrection, the power of redemption, the
power of salvation, the power to enact laws
for the carrying out and accomplishment
of His design. Both life and immortality
are brought to light as the gospel is
introduced, and He becomes
the Author of eternal life
and exaltation."
(John Taylor).

July 19

"They
grope in the
dark without light."
(Job 12:25).

The
Apostle Paul
tells us that "faith
is the substance of things
hoped for, the evidence of things
not seen." (Hebrews 11:1). Faith is not
to receive a sign from heaven. As Alma told
the Zoramites: "If a man knoweth a thing he hath
no cause to believe, for he knoweth it." (Alma 32:18). In
this context, if a sign is given before faith has transformed
us, we might have a sure knowledge of the event, but there
has been no expenditure of faith to create it. However, under
the proper circumstances, by doing our duty, our faith can
increase until it has blossomed into perfect knowledge.
Initially, then, faith is to believe what we do not
see, but its indescribable reward is to
see what we believe.

July 20

"And
they did also
carry with them
deseret, which, by
interpretation, is
a honey bee."
(Ether 2:3).

DSRT enjoyed a
ritual prominence within the
ancient culture of Egypt, and it was
very closely associated with the symbol of
the bee. Deseret now implies industry, as the
church and kingdom overcome everything
opposed to the economy of heaven. Isaiah
foresaw such a society, prophesying
that "they shall build houses, and
inhabit them, and they shall
plant vineyards, and eat
the fruit of them."
(Isaiah 65:21).

July 21

"Whosoever
committeth sin is
the servant of sin."
(John 8:34).

In most Western societies, the
rising generation faces unprecedented
challenges, as Satan makes a full frontal assault
on virtue and chastity. The new morality is intolerant,
exploitative, and oriented toward intercourse and not life. The
unity that couples seek cannot be accomplished at the pelvic level.
Other virtues such as honesty and integrity are no longer held in
high esteem. "Now we are a people of contention with strident
and accusatory voices heard in argument across the nation.
We spend millions of our resources in litigation against
one another. Our spiritual power is sapped by a
storm surge of pornography, by a debilitating
epidemic of the use of drugs that destroy
both body and mind. In all too many
ways, we have substituted human
sophistry for the Almighty."
(Gordon B. Hinckley).

July 22

"Sing unto the
Lord, all the earth."
(1 Chronicles 16:23).

Whether or not
we have paused for long
enough during our distracted
journey through life to consciously
appreciate it, each of us is completely
enveloped in a heavenly light. Helen Keller
wrote: "Keep your face to the sunshine, and you
cannot see the shadow." The shadow will still exist,
but if we are oriented toward the light, it will always be
behind us, out of sight, and out of mind. Light can give us
courage to transforms timidity and temerity into powerful
presence of mind. Light becomes a platform for assertive
action, empowering us with boldness. It charges us with
an intense and compellingly positive energy to meet
challenges. In the fight or flight scenario, it is light
that energizes the launch pad in preparation for
the adrenalin rush that propels us beyond the
threat. It provides the physical foundation
upon which is built our character, and its
luminescent trajectory can be traced to
an unfailing source that is nothing
less than a celestial dynamo.

July 23

"One thing thou
lackest. Go thy way, sell
whatsoever thou hast, and
give to the poor, and thou shalt
have treasure in heaven; and
come, take up the cross,
and follow me."
(Mark 10:21).

We
deny
ourselves of
all ungodliness,
when we take up the
cross. The vivid imagery
of Christ laboring along the
Via Dolorosa toward Calvary
helps us to remember that we
will never walk alone, even
though we may have been
required at times to bear
heavy burdens upon
our shoulders.

July 24

"Truth shall spring out of the earth, and righteousness shall look down from heaven." (Psalms 85:11).

Aside from the clear reference to the plates deposited in the Hill Cumorah, "out of the ground" and "low out of the dust" could also refer to ancient records of lost civilizations known only to God. Of one such ancient empire, the Israeli paleologist who unearthed Masada observed: "Nothing remains here today of the Romans but a heap of stones in the desert." What tales those rocks would tell, if they could but speak!

July 25

"As the
clay is in the
potter's hand, so
are ye in mine hand,
O house of Israel."
(Jeremiah 18:6).

In the
dim recesses
of memory before
time itself existed, God
created order and stability out
of chaos. It was Brigham Young's
belief that "all organized existence is
in progress either to endless advancement
in eternal perfections, or back to dissolution.
There is no period in the eternities wherein"
His creations "will become stationary,"
that they are "unable to advance in
knowledge, wisdom, power,
and glory."

July 26

"This is none other but the
house of God, and this is
the gate of heaven."
(Genesis 28:17).

During our eye-opening
journey through mortality, we often
brush up against the inviting portals of heaven
without even realizing we have done so. Helen Keller
"asked a friend who had just returned from a long walk in
the woods what she had observed. 'Nothing in particular,'
she replied. How was that possible, I asked myself? I, who
cannot hear or see, find hundreds of things to interest me
through mere touch. I feel the delicate symmetry of
a leaf. I pass my hands lovingly about the rough
shaggy bark of a pine. Occasionally, if I am
very fortunate, I place my hand gently
on a small tree and feel the happy
quiver of a bird in full song."
("The Atlantic Monthly").

July 27

"I will stand
before thee there
upon the rock in Horeb.
And thou shalt smite the
rock, and there shall come
water out of it, that the
people may drink."
(Exodus 17:6).

Even obediently
faithful Latter-day Saints
sometimes thoughtlessly exercise
unrighteous dominion, meaning that
they take strength unto themselves, rather
than giving God the credit and the glory for
their deeds. Indeed, when Moses asked Israel
at Horeb: "Must we fetch you water out of
this rock? he had a pronoun problem of
cosmic proportion!" (Numbers 20:10).
(Neal A. Maxwell).

July 28

"If thou
faint in the
day of adversity,
thy strength is small."
(Proverbs 24:10).

There are none of
us who will have the desire
or the capacity to partake of the
delicious fruit of everlasting life if we
have not first accepted the proposition
that perspiration precedes inspiration.
Capitulating to mediocrity or choosing
placation, rationalization, things of the
world, selfish pleasures, the honors of
men, or disobedience, suggests that
our priorities are out of order. As
long as we remain in this state,
we cannot generate the power
that is necessary to progress
along the path that leads
beyond that great and
spacious building all
the way to the
tree of life.

July 29

"He
maketh his sun
to rise on the evil
and on the good, and
sendeth rain on the just
and on the unjust."
(Matthew 5:45).

"Why is it,"
asked the poet, "that
whenever I reach for the sky to
climb aboard cloud nine, it evaporates
and rains upon my dreams? Is it a matter of
science, or simply a matter of fact, that not
even a cloud with a silver lining can hold
the weight of our dreams without some
precipitation? I think I've found the
answer to this dilemma. Keep on
reaching for the sky, but don't
forget your umbrella."
(Susan Stephenson).

July 30

"Then shall
the tongue of
the dumb sing."
(Isaiah 35:6).

"Jesus Christ (is)
the Son of God, (and)
the Father of heaven and
earth, the Creator of all things."
(Mosiah 3:8). Reverently, we take
His name upon ourselves, called by
the name of Christ in a familial way.
"He hath spiritually begotten you,"
taught Benjamin. (Mosiah 5:7). This
singular family relationship is the
reserve of the faithful, and it is in
addition to the incontrovertible
reality that every one of us is
a spirit child, created by our
Father in Heaven. It seems
that, within the blueprint
of the Plan, it has been
preordained that the
universe truly is a
machine whose
purpose is for
the making
of gods.

July 31

"The right hand of the Lord is exalted. The right hand of the Lord doeth valiantly."
(Psalms 118:16).

It has always been with the use of the right hand that the faithful have symbolized righteousness, and have demonstrated the power that comes with obedience to law. The Lord Himself testified that it was He who "laid the foundation of the earth, and (whose) right hand hath spanned the heavens." (1 Nephi 20:13). The right hand is used to ratify the validity of the sacred ordinances of the priesthood, in a symbolic gesture of the power of God that flows to us through His ordained administrators as they lay their own hands upon our heads to confer blessings, privileges, rights, and responsibilities.

August 1

"Why beholdest
thou the mote that is
in thy brother's eye,
but considerest not
the beam that is in
thine own eye?"
(Matthew 7:3).

To
righteously
endure to the end
may only oblige the
mastery of nothing more
than two simple principles:
repentance for our own sins,
and our forgiveness of others for
perceived injustices. Without these,
the Plan of Deliverance from Death is
rendered inoperative. These heavenly
characteristics are requirements of all
those who have a hope of inheriting
glory in the Celestial Kingdom. As
the Savior told Joseph Smith: "I,
the Lord, will forgive whom I
will forgive, but of you it is
required to forgive all
men" (D&C 64:10).

August 2

When the
Day of Judgment
arrives, as it surely will
for each one of us, the wicked
"shall be tormented with fire and
brimstone in the presence of
the holy angels, and in the
presence of the Lamb."
(Revelation 14:10).

The
fate of
the wicked
is a symbolical
representation not
to be taken literally.
Figuratively speaking, a
hardening of one's heart is
symptomatic of a debilitating
illness that, if left untreated, will
kill the spirit. The resultant cesspool
of nauseating brimstone effectively
smothers, because of its stench,
a fire that will not "dwell in
unholy temples."
(Alma 7:21).

August 3

"I saw
another angel
fly in the midst of
heaven, having the
everlasting gospel to
preach unto them that
dwell on the earth."
(Revelation 14:6).

The multitudes
of the angelic host who have
come down from the throne of God to
visit the earth have included Moroni and
John the Baptist, as well as Peter, James and
John. As messengers of Jesus Christ, they have
restored true doctrine. Because of the ministry of
these and other servants, a prophet has been able
to confidently declare that "no power on earth or
hell can overthrow or defeat that which God has
decreed. Every plan of the adversary will fail,
for the Lord knows the secret thoughts of
men, and sees the future with a vision
clear and perfect, even as though
it were in the past." (Joseph
Fielding Smith, Jr.).

August 4

"A double minded
man is unstable in
all his ways."
(James 1:8).

Both vanity
and pride distract us
from concentration on eternal
principles and create a conundrum
that is of cosmic proportion. We cannot
simultaneously concentrate on two things of
contrasting value. In prayer, our faith competes with
timidity; first blessing, and only later cursing, escapes the
same tongue, and devotion to God clashes with allegiance to
Babylon. Zion embodies substance. Babylon is transparent. Zion
preaches repentance; Babylon whines with rationalization. Zion
changes from the inside; Babylon from the outside. Zion acts,
while Babylon is acted upon. Conflicting thought processes
illustrate how Zion is grounded on a bedrock of standards,
while Babylon confuses values for principles. Its vanity
and pride project a false sense of carnal security.
It thinks that all is well in "Zion," even as the
world comes crashing down, like a train
wreck in slow motion. Mention of
the two deadly sins of 'vanity'
and 'pride' is found over
250 times in the
scriptures.

August 5

"He beheld
upon the ground a
round ball of curious
workmanship, and it
was of fine brass."
(1 Nephi 16:10).

It was the
Liahona that guided
the way to the Promised
Land. Transliteration from the
Hebrew suggests that "Liahona"
means "God gives light, as does the
sun." Notwithstanding that magnetic
compasses show the way we might go,
the Liahona was more than that; it was
a spiritual compass that pointed to the
way we should go. God has provided
for each of us the celestial compass
of gospel principles founded on
truth to guide us to safe haven
before the day of reckoning.
It is there for those who
have lost their way, to
bring them back to
the fold of the
Shepherd.

August 6

Babylon's
"plagues come in one
day; death, and mourning,
and famine; and she shall be
utterly burned with fire, for
strong is the Lord God
who judgeth her."
(Revelation 18:8).

Shortly
before the end
of the world, when
the Spirit is withdrawn,
there will be fires, tempests,
and vapors of smoke in foreign
lands, and wars, rumors of wars,
and earthquakes in sundry places.
(See Mormon 8:29-30). For nations
shall rise up against each other,
and kingdom against kingdom.
(See Matthew 24:6-7). In the
end, the consumption that
has been decreed will
make "a full end
of all nations."
(D&C 87:6).

August 7

"They
that feared
the Lord spake
often one to another;
and the Lord hearkened,
and heard it, and a book of
remembrance was written
before him, for them that
feared the Lord."
(Malachi 3:16).

Not long after
the death of her soul-mate,
Eve is reported to have exhorted
her children: "Hearken unto me, and
make tables of stone and others of clay, to
write on them about my life and your father's
that ye have heard and seen from us. If, by
water, the Lord judge our race, the tables
of clay will be dissolved and the tables
of stone will remain; but if, by fire,
the tables of clay will be baked
hard, and the tables of stone
will be broken up." (Book
of Adam and Eve – the
Pseudepigrapha).

August 8

"And when the
chief Shepherd shall
appear, ye shall receive
a crown of glory that
fadeth not away."
(1 Peter 5:4).

Each
day, we are 24
hours closer to what will
be the Pleasing Bar of Christ, if
we have patterned our behavior after
the Thirteenth Article of Faith. "We believe
in being honest, true, chaste, benevolent, virtuous,
and in doing good to all men. Indeed, we may say that we
follow the admonition of Paul: We believe all things, we hope
all things, we have endured many things, and hope to be able to
endure all things. If there is anything that is virtuous, lovely, or
of good report or praiseworthy, we seek after these things."
Marion D. Hanks observed that when we attend "the
banquet of consequences, there will not be much
that is satisfying at the table, unless we are
able to bow our heads in reverence,
and not hang them in shame, in
the presence of God, who
will be there."

August 9

"Awake
ye drunkards,
and weep."
(Joel 1:5).

In addition to
an apple a day, we all
need to have a daily dose of
truth, so that as we enjoy palpable
spiritual experiences, it will be as if the
veil before our eyes has become transparent.
We will feel clear, and whole, and at peace with
ourselves and our environment. Truth will permit us
to reach out and touch eternity. We will hold certainty in
our hands. Guiding principles will resonate with reality,
allowing us to move along an illuminated pathway to
our dreams. It is no wonder that Satan tries to cloud
our vision with the glitz and glamour of carnal
counterfeits that are really nothing more than
optical and spiritual illusions. His "foolish
fire," or will-o-the-wisp fictions, cannot
stand the heat of the mid-day sun;
they wither and die when they
are confronted by doctrine
and principles that have
been vigorously
activated by
agency.

August 10

"And they
said one to another,
did not our heart burn
within us, while he talked
with us by the way, and
while he opened to us
the scriptures?"
(Luke 24:32).

Enos said:
"And while I was
thus struggling in the
spirit, behold, the voice of
the Lord came into my mind."
(Enos 1:10). When voices come
as a flow of pure intelligence
that is attended by a burning
in the bosom, it is of God. A
search for external warrant
is really nothing more than
our entrenched desire to
receive confirmations
regarding intuitions
that we already
have felt.

August 11

"If we do
not improve
our time while in
this life, then cometh
the night of darkness,
wherein there can be no
labor performed."
(Alma 34:33).

Out of the distant past
of mid-nineteenth century America,
the warning of Daniel Webster ominously echoes
in our ears: "If we and our posterity shall be true to the
Christian religion, and if we and they shall live always in the
fear of God and shall respect his commandments, we may have
the highest hopes for the future fortunes of our country. It will
have no decline and fall, but it will go on prospering. But, if
we or our posterity shall reject religious instructions and
authority, violate the rules of morality and recklessly
destroy the political constitution which holds us
together, no man can tell how sudden a
catastrophe may overwhelm us,
that shall bury all of our
glory in profound
obscurity."

August 12

"Be of
good courage, and
let us behave ourselves
valiantly for our people, and
for the cities of our God, and
let the Lord do that which
is good in his sight."
(1 Chronicles 19:3).

If we
are true
to our moral
compass, and have
courage, we will not jostle
with others for the best seat in
first class on the temptation train to
hell. Elder Neal A. Maxwell said: "If we
pause at every spur on the road, to explore
every detour from the strait and narrow path,
to get our ticket punched, as it were, by every
uninformed skeptic whose personal agenda
includes matters that we would normally
dismiss as trivial, we risk weakening
our faith in the foundation
principles" of the
gospel.

August 13

Do not "be
wearied and faint
in your minds."
(Hebrews 12:3).

During its genesis,
our "faith is not to have a perfect
knowledge of things; therefore if (we) have
faith, (we) hope for things which are not seen, which
are true." (Alma 30: 21). Faith is unnecessary, if its object
is demonstrable to our physical senses. Faith, then, is not to
have a perfect knowledge of things gained through our own
experiences. Korihor's demand for a sign was the condition
of his faith, since he trusted only his physical senses. This
rational approach is the enemy of faith. Thus, secular
humanism and other similar corrupted ideologies
destroy faith and are devilish doctrines, subtle
though they may be. They are abominable to
God because they thwart the successful
execution of His Plan, by denying
the efficacy of saving faith,
which is a commendable
thing in the sight
of God.

August 14

"Let
us (put) on
the breastplate
of faith and love,
and for an helmet,
the hope of salvation."
(1 Thessalonians 5:8).

As
long as we are
sure that we never
cease to make consistent
deposits to our spiritual bank
accounts throughout the years, it
is not very likely that they will be
overdrawn during times of need.
In moments of crisis, the Savior
will call upon these bounteous
reserves to calm our troubled
souls. With David, we will
exclaim: Thou anointest
my head with oil. My
cup runneth over."
(Psalms 23:5).

August 15

"I know
thy works, that
thou art neither cold
nor hot. I would thou
wert cold or hot."
(Revelation 3:15).

We have been
endowed with a special
commission from our Father,
which is the solemn responsibility
to become intimately familiar with the
principles embedded within the doctrine
of His Plan of Redemption. This must be so,
because, in the final analysis, we cannot hope
to find lasting happiness, except we comply with
the unambiguous rules of conduct with which it is
associated. As Joseph Smith counseled: "Happiness is
the object and design of our existence, and will be the
end thereof, if we pursue the path that leads to it, and
this path is virtue, uprightness, faithfulness, holiness,
and keeping all the commandments of God." To do
anything else is vanity, and for Saints who ought
to know better, it is blasphemous to act in ways
that are incompatible with the principles that
pointedly promote the laws of the Celestial
Kingdom. Those who embrace that reality
will discover that it is the only setting
wherein it is possible for them to
receive a fullness of joy
in the eternities
to come.

August 16

"The
Lord is nigh
unto them that are
of a broken heart, and
saveth such as be of
a contrite spirit."
(Psalms 34:18).

When we have
internalized the quality
of contrition, our lives enjoy
an expansion of opportunity into
new dimensions. We see things differently.
Suddenly, good outweighs evil, love overcomes
jealousy, hate, and prejudice, light drives out darkness,
knowledge banishes ignorance, humility displaces pride,
courtesy overwhelms rudeness, appreciation overpowers
thanklessness, abundance supersedes poverty, well-being
replaces weakness, simplicity overshadows perplexity,
harmony supplants discord, faith subdues fear, hope
casts out despair, charity ousts selfishness, joy
deposes unhappiness, sadness, dejection,
and misery, confidence is substituted
for timidity, certainty dethrones
bewilderment, and assurance
unseats discouragement
and even despair.

August 17

"Blessed is the man that endureth temptation, for when he is tried, he shall receive the crown of life, which the Lord hath promised to them that love him."
(James 1:12).

The message of the Restoration is that it is possible for each of us not just to resist evil, but also to live abundantly by tapping into unlimited reserves of living water that are waiting for us in an inexhaustible aquifer. "These currents and many more are part of the flowing fountain of the church. If we do not drink, but if we die of thirst while only inches away from the fountain, the fault comes down to us. For the free, full, flowing, living water is there." (Truman Madsen). We discover the source of David's strength from a careful study of his 23rd psalm. It was his cup of living water, he said, that "runneth over."
(Psalms 23:5).

August 18

"O
Lord, thou
art our father. We
are the clay, and thou
our potter, and we
all are the work
of thy hand."
(Isaiah 64:8).

"If
you
can leave
your students
with one principal
commitment in response
to the Savior's incomparable
sacrifice for them, His payment for
their transgressions, and His sorrow for
their sins, leave with them the necessity
to obey; to yield in their own difficult
domain and hours of decision to the
will of the Father, whatever the
cost." (Jeffrey Holland).

August 19

"Endless
punishment is
God's punishment."
(D&C 19:12).

One of the
inherent dangers
that is associated with
a shallow understanding of
principles is that we risk being
blind-sided, and then falling into
transgression and finally suffering
the inevitable consequences of our
poor choices. We have all witnessed
how picking apart the scriptures can
distort the doctrines into nonsensical
fragments with little or no coherent
connection. The wicked inhabitants
of Ammonihah were counseled by
Alma: "Behold, the scriptures are
before you. If ye will wrest
them it shall be to your
own destruction."
(Alma 13:20).

August 20

"Then shall
the dust return to the
earth as it was, and the
spirit shall return unto
God who gave it."
(Ecclesiastes 12:7).

When our dust finally
returns to mother earth that
gave it, we will have completed a
full circle back to our Maker, Who is the
the Fashioner of the universe itself. And so,
in all our attempts to comprehend the cosmos,
we will finally realize that we were just trying to
understand ourselves. Every heavy element in our
bodies, including the calcium in our bones and the
iron in the hemoglobin of our blood, was created in
the cataclysm of a supernova. When we ask about
the origin of the universe and its destiny, we are
quite simply probing humanity's fundamental
questions, that include: 'Where did we come
from, why are we here,' and perhaps that
most important query of all, 'where are
we going?' In a coming day, we will be
reintroduced to the land that existed
before time "when meadow, grove,
and stream, the earth, and every
common sight, did seem to be
appareled in celestial light."
(William Wordsworth).

August 21

"For Christ sent
me not to baptize, but to
preach the gospel; not with
wisdom of words, lest the
cross of Christ should be
made of none effect."
(1 Corinthians 1:17).

The
Apostle Paul
used the imagery of
the cross to impress upon
our minds the doctrine of the
Atonement. Its symbolism is found
in the ordinance of the Sacrament, where
the faithful take upon themselves the name
of Christ, and promise to always remember
Him, and keep His commandments. This
sacred rite permits them to enjoy in
greater abundance the godly
qualities of unimpaired
innocence and
virtue.

August 22

"Some
(seeds) fell upon
stony places, where
they had not much earth.
And some fell among thorns;
and the thorns sprung up, and
choked them. But others fell
unto good ground, and
brought forth fruit."
(Matthew 13:5-8).

Belief is a
mental assent to the
truth, without the moral
element of responsibility that
we call faith. To those to whom
much is given, however, more
is expected. The gift of faith
requires action. Therefore,
"faith without works is
dead, being alone."
(James 2:17).

August 23

"They
are drunken,
but not with wine;
they stagger, but not
with strong drink."
(Isaiah 29:9).

The scriptures
warn us in unmistakable
language that a deadly threat to
our temporal and spiritual welfare
exists. It is hidden in a time bomb called
pride, ready to explode and scatter its lethal
contents among the people in a deadly deluge of
deception. The warning applies especially to those
who are trying to move beyond an outward law of
carnal commandments to the internalization of a
higher standard of behavior that is powered by
the Holy Ghost, Whose presence demands of
true disciples a celestial criterion, where
humility quietly reigns.

August 24

"Awake, awake,
stand up, O Jerusalem,
which hast drunk at the
hand of the Lord the
cup of his fury."
(Isaiah 51:17).

For far too long,
Israel has "drunk of the
dregs of the cup of trembling." (2
Nephi 8:23). At last, she will put on her
strength by exercising the authority of the
Holy Priesthood of God. As Moroni exhorted:
"Awake, and arise from the dust, O Jerusalem; yea,
and put on thy beautiful garments, O daughter of
Zion; and strengthen thy stakes, and enlarge thy
borders forever, that thou mayest no more be
confounded, that the covenants of the
Eternal Father which he hath made
unto thee, O house of Israel,
may be fulfilled."
(Moroni 10:31).

August 25

"What shall I
do, that I may
be born of God,
having this wicked
spirit rooted out of my
breast, and receive His
spirit, that I may be
filled with joy?"
(Alma 22:15).

"Please teach by the Holy Spirit," Jeffrey Holland urged those who would shepherd the Saints. "Give your students the opportunity for a spiritual experience in every way you can. That is the message of the Gospels. It is the message of all scripture. These spiritual experiences, recorded in those sacred writings, will help keep others on track, and in the church in our day, just as similar experiences did for those members in New Testament times."

August 26

"I have
trodden the winepress alone,
and of the people there was none
with me. For I will tread them in mine
anger, and trample them in my fury;
and their blood shall be sprinkled
upon my garments, and I will
stain all my raiment."
(Isaiah 63:3).

Who
has trod the
winepress alone,
and would not allow the
bitter cup to pass from Him?
My Exemplar and my Redeemer,
our Lord and Savior Jesus Christ, was
He Who did not shrink from the olive press,
from the agonizing solitude of the spiritual
self-sufficiency demanded by Justice but
only made possible by Mercy, that
was required of Him by His
Father in the Garden
of Gethsemane.

August 27

"Whosoever shall
smite thee on thy right cheek,
turn to him the other also."
(Matthew 5:39).

The Lord invites us to experience
benevolent blindness, to turn the other cheek
and to go the second mile, because He knows that
the process by which discipline is developed requires not
only probing our strengths, but also testing our weakness and
extending our boundaries. We receive confirmation, as feelings
of self-confidence grow and tentative overtures are replaced by
purposeful actions. Our discipleship is intimately bound to
righteousness. The way is strait, but Heavenly Father has
provided us with a wide range of experiences because
His belief in our capacity to adhere to the Plan, when
faced with adversity, is unwavering. Our reward,
although it may now be only dimly perceived,
in a coming day will be unmistakably
plain. 'Well done, thou good and
faithful servant. Enter into the
presence of the Lord!'
will ring in our
ears.

August 28

"Jesus, when he was baptized,
went up straightway out of the water.
And lo, the heavens were opened unto
him, and he saw the Spirit of God
descending like a dove, and
lighting upon him."
(Matthew 3:16).

The
inimitable image
of a dove has always
been associated with the
spirit of peace. The prophet
Joseph Smith explained that the
sign of the dove is an emblem or a
token of truth and innocence. After
our cleansing in the shining waters
of purification, it comes at the time
of the second baptism, when we
are justified with fire and
by the Holy Ghost.

August 29

"Wherefore,
dig about them,
and prune them, and
dung them once more,
for the last time."
(Jacob 5:64).

To dung
a plant, that is to
say, to spread manure
around its base, is symbolic
of the nourishing of gathered
Israel with the restored gospel.
This careful attention will cause
her to grow, or to increase in her
righteousness, as God nurtures
His children one last time in
anticipation of the return
and millennial reign of
their rightful King,
the Lord of both
heaven and
earth.

August 30

"Verily I say unto
thee, thou shalt by no
means come out thence,
till thou hast paid the
uttermost farthing."
(Matthew 5:26).

"It is the duty of
nations as well as of men
to owe their dependence upon
the over-ruling power of God, to
confess their sins and transgressions
in humble sorrow. Yet with assured
hope that genuine repentance will
lead to mercy and pardon, (we)
recognize that those nations
only are blessed whose
God is the Lord."
(Abe Lincoln).

August 31

"He that overcometh, the
same shall be clothed
in white raiment."
(Revelation 3:5).

During the early
Middle Ages, the White
Martyrs of Christian Ireland
clothed themselves in distinctive
white woolen robes, and fanned out
across Europe. In dozens of locations,
they founded monasteries. Their influence
across the continent is incalculable. They
reestablished literacy, and breathed new
life into the exhausted cultures of
Europe. "And that is how the
Irish saved civilization."
(Thomas Cahill).

September 1

"Your gold and
silver is cankered; and
the rust of them shall be a
witness against you, and
shall eat your flesh
as it were fire."
(James 5:3).

"Do
you have any
money?" is Satan's
golden question. He
wants us to believe that we
can have anything in this world,
for money. Does a need exist? Solve
the problem with a generous application
of money, to be repeated in equal doses four
times a day, for life. This is the prescription upon
which the wicked rely, but it shifts the blame for
the world's worries from their shoulders to the
availability of temporal resources, in a flight
from personal accountability. As Babylon
demands undeserved entitlement, Zion
quietly embraces the work ethic. The
irrational behavior of Babylon is
simply the expression of its
juvenile irresponsibility,
in contrast to Zion's
spiritual stability.

September 2

"And
he gave unto
Moses two tables
of testimony, tables
of stone, written with
the finger of God.
(Exodus 31:18).

The
Word of
the Lord, the
Decalogue, has
been written in the
fleshy tables of my new
heart. (See 2 Corinthians 3:3).
The Ten Commandments have
become the spiritual formulary
of the anti-rejection medication
that I know that I must take on
a daily basis, for as long as I
want to live in the light of
His love and feel the
warmth of His
embrace.

September 3

"Except the Lord build the house, they labour in vain that build it. Except the Lord keep the city, the watchman waketh but in vain."
(Psalms 127:1).

The Saints view the commandments as a consummate compilation of affirmative actions. They are committed by covenant to a lifestyle that is centered on Christ. Members of His church find that the relationship between commandments and blessings is directly proportional. They have learned that it is impossible to have one without the other. It is only this perspective that makes any sense of the expression that His yoke is easy and His burden is light. It is no wonder His message has been characterized as the gospel of repentance, and that we are encouraged to rely upon His merits, that are exemplified by the greatest blessing of all; and that is His Infinite Atonement.

September 4

"I also
cast my eyes
round about, and
beheld, on the other side
of the river of water, a great
and spacious building, and it
stood as it were in the air,
high above the earth."
(1 Nephi 8:26).

A powerful
illustration of the pride
and the vain imaginations of
the world is manifest in the great
and spacious building that was seen
by Lehi, in vision. Such a description
matched precisely the appearance of
cities to desert dwellers. Those who
made their homes in tents always
felt uneasy in cities, with their
mortar and stone, and were
often made to feel inferior
by the more worldly
denizens of the
metropolitan
milieu.

September 5

"For unto
us a child is born,
unto us a son is given;
and the government shall
be upon his shoulder, and his
name shall be called Wonderful,
Counselor, The Mighty God, The
Everlasting Father, (and)
The Prince of Peace."
(Isaiah 9:6).

The
day is now at
hand when "every
ear shall hear it, and
every knee shall bow, and
every tongue shall confess"
that Jesus is the Christ. (D&C
88:104). He will be recognized
as the "Lord of lords, and King
of kings." (Rev. 17:14). When we
invite Him to come and dwell in
our hearts, He becomes not only
the finisher of our faith but also
the author of our spiritual
regeneration, as well as
the poet laureate of
our Heavenly
Father.

September 6

"And I heard
the voice of the Lord."
(Isaiah 6:8).

It is never an
easy thing to explain
to the uninitiated how the
Lord speaks to His children. "The
wind bloweth where it listeth, and thou
hearest the sound thereof, but canst not tell
whence it cometh, and whither it goeth. So is
every one that is born of the Spirit." (John 3:8).
He said that His words "are not of men, nor of
man, but of me. Wherefore, you shall testify they
are of me, and not of man. For it is my voice which
speaketh them unto you; for they are given by my
Spirit unto you, and by my power you can read
them one to another; and save it were by my
power you could not have them. Wherefore
you can testify that you have heard my
voice, and know my words."
(D&C 18: 34-36).

September 7

"The Son of
God hath atoned for
original guilt, wherein the sins
of the parents cannot be answered
upon the heads of the children,
for they are whole from the
foundation of the world."
(Moses 6:54).

The
Atonement of
the Son of God, Who
loved little children, was
worked out to the last detail
before the foundation of the world.
Confident in His ability to muster His
spiritual reserves to save mankind, Jesus
Christ led the way for all who would take
up their cross and follow Him along the
path leading through the Garden of
Gethsemane, to the court of Pilate,
along the Via Dolorosa, to the
hill of Calvary, to an empty
tomb, and on to eternal
life in the Celestial
Kingdom.

September 8

"Arise, and be baptized, and wash away thy sins, calling on the name of the Lord."
(Acts 22:16).

The Atonement of our Lord and Savior Jesus Christ has the power to bless each of our lives with a new beginning, even a rebirth. Our baptism, for example, eliminates the stain of sin that has been accumulating since the age of accountability. "Inasmuch as ye were born into the world by water, and blood, and the Spirit, which I have made, and so became of dust a living soul, even so ye must be born again into the kingdom of heaven, of water, and of the Spirit, and be cleansed by blood, even the blood of mine Only Begotten."
(Moses 6:59).

September 9

"And the
God of peace shall
bruise Satan under
your feet, shortly."
(Romans 16:20).

As Alexander
Pope observed long ago,
so does it ring true even today, that
"vice is a monster of so frightful mien, as to be
hated needs but to be seen. Yet seen too oft, familiar
with her face, we first endure, then pity, then embrace."
We must recognize that it is easier to hold up an umbrella
than it is to turn off the rain. In our communities, it seems
that immorality is often legislated. When this happens, it
takes on a legitimacy it has neither earned nor deserves.
Since wickedness cannot be summarily eliminated,
the faithful must take whatever measures are
necessary to control damage, as quickly
as possible. A stiff dose of gospel
principles is the best remedy,
together with a dash of
sackcloth and
ashes.

September 10

"Ye
have heard
that antichrist
shall come."
(1 John 2:18).

Anti-Christ is one
who openly rebels against
the Lord, and actively opposes
Him. He may establish himself or any
other person or system as a substitute for the
Savior, and then seek to promote that alternative
agenda. With a perverted, twisted reason, Anti-Christ
attempts to overthrow true doctrine by preaching things that
are flattering to the people. He often has formidable skills and
weapons in his arsenal, but like the sophist, he is an intellectual
guerilla, insisting on fighting his battles on his own turf and
according to his own rules. He uses the persuasiveness of
his dramatic oratory skills, his polished rhetoric, and
the siren song of seduction, as his most effective
armaments, and they are typically economical
in terms of tangible benefits. He has found
that he does not need to use expensive
high velocity large caliber armor
piercing rounds in order to
effectively kill the spirit.
Fiery darts of vanity
seem to do the
trick.

September 11

"And thy heaven
that is over thy head
shall be brass, and the earth
that is under thee shall be iron."
(Deuteronomy 28:23).

When our
Lord and Savior
Jesus Christ returns, He
will come in power, alluding to
His personal righteousness. He will
come in dominion, suggesting priesthood
authority. He will come in glory, worthy of
the inner peace that righteousness brings.
He will come in majesty, which implies
that Christ is King of all the earth, that
He wields all power and is in control
of all things. He will come in might,
which means that His strength is
more than enough to vanquish
Satan and to establish His
own dominion, that is
the Kingdom of
God, on the
earth.

September 12

"Thou art obstinate, and thy neck is an iron sinew, and thy brow brass."
(Isaiah 48:4).

Those who are characterized as being stiff-necked have skin that is so thick and calloused that extraordinary measures are required to penetrate it in order to to touch their spirits. As Enos reported of his people: "There was nothing save it was exceeding harshness, preaching, and prophesying of wars, and contentions, and destructions, and continually reminding them of death, and the duration of eternity, and the judgments and the power of God, and all these things, stirring them up continually to keep them in the fear of the Lord; I say there was nothing short of these things, and exceedingly great plainness of speech, would keep them from going down speedily to destruction."
(Enos 1:23).

September 13

"He laid hold on the
dragon, that old serpent,
which is the Devil, and
Satan, and bound him
a thousand years."
(Revelation 20:2).

When we defy
Satan by standing up to
him and remaining true to our
covenants, He gets angry, as he was
with Moses, during their confrontation on
"an exceedingly high mountain," so long ago.
(Moses 1:1). On that occasion, he cried with a loud
voice, trembled, and shook, but then departed from the
great lawgiver, who remained resolute at that pivotal point
in his personal progress. Things will be different during the
Millennium, however. "Because of the righteousness of his
people" who remain on the earth during the thousand
years of peace, Satan will be bound, "wherefore, he
cannot be loosed for the space of many years; for
he hath no power over the hearts of the people,
for they dwell in righteousness, and the
Holy One of Israel reigneth."
(1 Nephi 22:26).

September 14

"Joseph is a fruitful bough, even a fruitful bough by a well, whose branches run over the wall."
(Genesis 49:22).

In an ancient parable that touches on our own day, Israel was likened unto an olive tree with many branches that had broken off, only to be "scattered upon all the face of the earth." (1 Nephi 10:12). Lehi learned from the Spirit that his family group would be one of those branches that would be led from its homeland at Jerusalem to its own land of promise, that it might personify the fruitful bough that had been prophesied by Jacob.

September 15

It is the
duty of the priests
"to administer bread
and wine, the emblems
of the flesh and (the)
blood of Christ."
(D&C 20:40).

When
I come to
Thy feast, may
I prostrate myself
before Thy face, and
with fasting and prayer,
strive to retain Thy favor.
In sackcloth and ashes, and
with the sacrifice of a broken
heart and a contrite spirit, let
me feel Thy tender mercies.
For Thou art strong, and I
am weak, Thou art great,
and I am nothing. Let
me never forget my
unworthiness
before Thy
face.

September 16

"And
they shall
come forth,
both small and
great, and all shall
stand before his bar."
(Mormon 9:13).

At the
end of the day,
we possess nothing
but our character, that
leaves each of us free to
tell our own story. It is a
record that cannot lie, for
it is written in the sinews
of our bodies as much as
it is in the tablets of our
minds. It is a narrative
that will be unfolded
before the throne of
God, where He will
ask, ever so gently
gently, for us to
supply every
one of the
details.

September 17

"The only begotten Son…is in the bosom of the Father." (John 1:18).

In order that He might put His love for us in terms that we can only begin to comprehend, the Lord explained: "I am the same which (has) taken the Zion of Enoch into mine own bosom." (D&C 38:4). To be "in one's bosom" is a Hebrew idiom derived from the fact that anciently, a man's clothing consisted of flowing robes, with a sash forming a space where treasured possessions, including children, were carried. The expression implies a very close and favored relationship.

September 18

"As arrows
are in the hand
of a mighty man, so
are children of the youth.
Happy is the man that hath
his quiver full of them."
(Psalms 127:4-5).

The
equations that
define marriage are
governed by an entirely
new set of variables when
that holy union has been blessed
with offspring. Those who avoid the
challenges and responsibilities of raising
children may have progressed beyond the
initial dependency stage of interpersonal
relationships, but they become mired in
the independency stage of maturation.
Without the added dimensions of
a family, how can they fully
enjoy the freedom that
interdependency
offers?

September 19

Those
who break their
covenants "shall be
delivered over to the
buffetings of Satan
until the day of
redemption."
(D&C 78:12).

My
consecrated
covenant with God
is ever before me as
I engage in the works
of Abraham. He is my
example. I shall follow
in the footsteps of the
Father of the Faithful.
I shall, forevermore,
enjoy the blessings
promised to his
righteous
seed.

September 20

"Take unto you the
whole armour of God."
(Ephesians 6:13).

As
we put on
His armour, we
press ever forward,
with complete dedication,
steadfastness, confidence, and
our firm determination in Christ,
with a perfect brightness of hope, or
flawless faith, and charity, or a love of
God, and of all men. When we do this,
not just casually sampling, but feasting
upon the words of Christ, enduring in
righteousness through this veil of
tears to the very end, we will
have eternal life, which
is the greatest gift
that God may
bestow.

September 21

"Wherever the carcass is,
there will the eagles be
gathered together."
(Matthew 24:28).

The Saints of every age,
who have experienced firsthand the
vicissitudes of persecution, have always
assembled in their holy places to prepare
their hearts that they might make ready all
things against the day when tribulation and
"desolation are sent forth upon the wicked."
(D&C 29:8). Where the body of the church
is found, therein will also lie the power of
the priesthood, creating an environment
that is sacred, consecrated, hallowed,
and sanctified; where honest effort
is recompensed by a hierarchy of
regularly recurring plateaus
of progress leading ever
upward to pinnacles
of perfection.

September 22

"Feast upon
the words of Christ."
(2 Nephi 32:3).

When it is
operating at full
capacity, the perpetual
motion machine that is the
dynamo of the gospel creates a
vigorously charged environment that
encourages change. During that process,
we are nourished at a smorgasbord where we
never become satiated. When our lives are in
harmony with gospel principles, we are in a
constant state of improvement leading to
perfection, as if we were experiencing
night after night the delights of a five
star restaurant, and awakening in
the morning with our spiritual
bodies even more fit and
trim than they had
been before.

September 23

"He leadeth them by the
neck with a flaxen cord, until
he bindeth them with his
strong chains forever."
(2 Nephi 26:22).

Before
he is able to
unceremoniously
drag them down to hell,
Satan gently places a flaxen
cord, that can actually feel quite
comfortable, around the throats of
the imprudent. But once inappropriate
behavior patterns have been established,
the unwary are unpleasantly surprised to
find that they have sacrificed their agency
to act independently, and they are bound
by the yoke of sin to engage in conduct
that is habitually self-defeating but is
very difficult to change. In this way
does the adversary bind us with
his strong chains forever, and
squeeze the last vestige of
celestial air from
our lungs.

September 24

"Some trust in chariots, and
some in horses, but we will
remember the name of
the Lord, our God."
(Psalms 20:7).

Father, I pray
Thee that when I am
wrong, I will be willing to
make changes, and when I am
right, that Thou wilt make it easy
for others to live with me. Strengthen
me, that the power of my influence will
far exceed the authority of my position.
Let me beware, lest I trust more in my
own abilities or talents than in Thy
omniscience and benevolence, or
in my capacity to determine my
fame, fortune, obscurity or
poverty. "Not as I will,
but as thou wilt."
(Matthew 26:39).

September 25

"Except
a man be born
again, he cannot see
the kingdom of God."
(John 3:3).

In the
modern day
state of Israel, those
who are known by the
name "Sabra" are the native
born children of the Covenant.
The fruit of the prickly pear cactus,
the sabra, has a dry and unappealing
skin. But inside, it is sweet, juicy, and
is pleasing to the taste. Just so, when
God measures us, He does not look
at our rough exteriors, but on the
inner vessels. He does not put
the measuring tape around
our heads, but instead
around our
hearts.

September 26

"And everyone that heareth
these saying of mine, and doeth
them not, shall be likened unto a
foolish man, which built his
house upon the sand."
(Matthew 7:27).

I am
less than
the dust of the
earth, but the quarry
from which I have built
my testimony is as Cephas.
My reinforcement is a solid
and enduring foundation
of stone upon which I
will strengthen my
faith, that it
might not
fail.

September 27

"Then
Samuel took
a vial of oil, and
poured it upon his
head, and kissed him."
(1 Samuel 10:1).

Elder Jeffrey Holland
encouraged the Saints, that they
might "try a little harder to fortify
others so powerfully that whatever
temptations the devil throws at them,
they will be able to withstand and thus
truly, in that moment, be free from evil.
Could we try a little harder," he asked,
"to teach so powerfully and spiritually
that we really help that individual
who walks alone, who lives
alone, who weeps in the
dark of the night?"
(Jeffrey Holland).

September 28

"I do set my bow
in the cloud, and it
shall be for a token of
a covenant between
me and the earth."
(Genesis 9:13).

Just as
God swore an oath
with Noah that He would
never again destroy the earth by a
flood, so did He likewise swear by His
prophet Isaiah that He would not be angry
with the children of Israel. "For the mountains
shall depart and the hills be removed, but my
kindness shall not depart from thee, neither
shall the covenant of my peace be
removed, saith the Lord that
hath mercy on thee."
(Isaiah 54:10).

September 29

"Oil for
the light, spices
for anointing oil, and
for sweet incense."
(Exodus 25:6).

Missionaries of
The Church of Jesus
Christ of Latter-day Saints
are agents of the Lord, and
dispense the oil of gladness by
bringing the knowledge of God to
all who will listen. Those who die
without the opportunity to obtain
this wisdom will yet be given a
chance to receive and accept
the gospel in the life after
death, so that they, too,
might become heirs
of the Celestial
Kingdom.

September 30

"Keep my
commandments
and live, and my
law as the apple
of thine eye."
(Proverbs 7:2).

"Those
who live in
daily thanksgiving
have a way of opening
their eyes to the wonders
and beauties of the world as
though seeing them for the first
time. They are usually among the
happiest people on the earth."
(Joseph Wirthlin).

October 1

"Now
they, after
being sanctified by
the Holy Ghost, having
their garments made white,
being pure and spotless before
God, could not look upon sin save
it were with abhorrence; and there
were many, exceedingly great many,
who were made pure and entered into
the rest of the Lord their God.
(Alma 13:12).

We read in
scripture that those
who have repented and
become the Lord's disciples
are figuratively characterized
as "white, fair, and beautiful."
(1 Nephi 13:5). Moroni used the
terms "spotless, pure, fair, and
white."(Mormon 9:6). These
are those who symbolically
have been cleansed by the
blood of the Lamb, in a
rite of purification as
old as time itself.

October 2

"Babylon the great is fallen, is fallen, and is become the habitation of devils." (Revelation 18:2).

Idumea's philosophy of selfish indulgence has become firmly entrenched in the wicked and idolatrous communities of the world, in the personification at one and the same time, of the "great whore that sitteth upon many waters, with whom the kings of the earth have committed fornication." (Revelation 17:1-2). This should not be surprising, inasmuch as it is the prince of darkness who rules Spiritual Babylon, the habitation of devils.

October 3

"We
will rejoice
in thy salvation,
and in the name of
our God we will set
up our banners."
(Psalms 20:5).

Each one of us is
a precious child of God who
has been invited to participate in
the quorums and auxiliaries through
which the Lord operates His church. But
it is only those who have become Saints, those
who are bound by its ordinances, who may receive
the promises and blessings of the gospel by means of
covenants of action between themselves and the Lord.
Ordinances attest to God's nature and they confirm
that The Church of Jesus Christ is founded on
unchanging principles. They bridge the
gulf between heaven and earth, and
illustrate that the requirements
for obtaining salvation are
the same for every
one of us.

October 4

"For a small moment have I forsaken thee, but with great mercies will I gather thee."
(Isaiah 54:7).

In the Last Days, as Israel is gathered from the far corners of the earth, individual members of The Church of Jesus Christ will ignite with the flame of faith as the Lord blesses them with the spiritual tools needed to tap into their potential. To reach God's kingdom, we must set our course, and then move along it. Our progression begins with small steps. "Life is a sheet of paper white, where each of us may write a line or two, and then comes night. Greatly begin. If thou hast time but for a line, make that sublime. Not failure, but low aim is crime."
(James Lowell).

October 5

"He cast upon them
the fierceness of his anger,
wrath, and indignation, and
trouble, by sending evil
angels among them."
(Psalms 78:49).

The terrible
indictment of the
wicked in the Last Days
is that they can have no claim
on the tender mercies of the Lord,
because they have either willfully or
ignorantly chosen to deny themselves the
blessings of the Atonement. In their case, the
Judgment has already taken place. They begin to
realize that it is a very unpleasant experience, as an
awful avalanche of consequences overwhelms them,
smothering any hope of timely deliverance. They will
have rolled the dice, counting on lady-luck, but they
will have lost everything in their ill-considered bet
with fate. When they are finally given over to the
buffetings of Satan, they will be permitted, on
their own initiative, to scrape together
their very last farthings, that they
might, somehow, pay for
their redemption.

October 6

"They have
corrupted themselves…
they are a perverse and
crooked generation."
(Deuteronomy 31:5).

The
world has an
insatiable desire for
telestially titillating fast
food that has been carelessly
prepared and impatiently heated
up in a sensory microwave oven. It can
only be superficially desirable, however,
because it has been saturated with empty
calories. When the unrepentant wicked
measure the messages delivered by the
missionaries, they see darkly, or only
through the hazy filter of a worldly
pollution. Their futile attempts to
whitewash the truth only reveal
the underlying sores that are a
corruption and a canker on
their character, that only
serves to blind them
even further to
the truth.

October 7

"Ye are
God's building."
(1 Corinthians 3:9).

Only when it stands upon a
solid religious foundation, will the
marriage partnership be transformed
into something much more than a social
convention with little incentive to make it
work. With faith, however, the relationship
between a man and a woman may become
almost sacramental. If partners view their
vows as sacred covenants with God, they
are more likely to be able to weather the
storms that will inevitably arise as their
relationship continues to develop with
maturity. Their devotions, that have
been anchored to shared religious
experience, can bind them to the
promise of kingdoms, thrones,
and principalities, let alone
powers, dominions, and
even to exaltations
in the Kingdom
of God.

October 8

"In that day,
shall the deaf hear the
words of the book, and the
eyes of the blind shall see
out of obscurity and
out of darkness."
(2 Nephi 27:29).

When
the threads that have
been woven into the conduct
of our lives conform to the pattern
that has been established by the Savior,
scales of darkness fall away and the eyes
of our spiritual understanding are opened
to the heavens. We attune our ears, that we
may comprehend the otherwise inaudible
whisperings of the Spirit, and our hearts
are stirred with the pure love of Christ
as we lose ourselves in service, with
compassion toward the needs of
our neighbors, 'though our
best efforts may remain
unappreciated.

October 9

The
Lord spoke
of "the mother of
abominations, that made
all nations drink of the wine of
the wrath of her fornication, that
persecuted the saints of God,
that shed her blood."
(D&C 88:94).

Satan
rules in his
dominion by the
subtle manipulation
of those whose focus is
on the worship idols. But
"priesthood is the legitimate
rule of God, and is the power
that has a right to rule upon the
earth, and when the will of God
is done on earth, as it is done
in heaven, no other power
will bear rule" in either
of those dominions.
(John Taylor).

October 10

"To him
that overcometh
will I give to eat of
the hidden manna."
(Revelation 2:17).

In our
discussions
with investigators
who mirror the spiritual
immaturity of the Zoramites,
we must never forget that they need
milk, and not meat, to nourish the quality
of their belief. The tender shoots that spring
from young testimonies need to be carefully
nurtured. Ecclesiastical embroidery often
unnecessarily complicates the stitchery
of the simple gospel messages that
we carry in our hearts, that we
wear on our coat sleeves,
and that come from
our lips.

October 11

"If I whet my
glittering sword,
and mine hand take
hold on judgment. I will
render vengeance to mine
enemies, and I will reward
them that hate me."
(Deuteronomy 32:41).

Although
there may be times
when we would like to be
able to step in and do so, we
do not make the rules. "God's
standard, the celestial standard, is
absolute and allows no exceptions.
There is no wiggle room. He cannot
allow moral or ethical imperfection
to dwell in His presence. He cannot
tolerate sin. The celestial standard
is complete innocence, pure and
simple, and nothing less will be
tolerated in His kingdom."
(Stephen Robinson).

October 12

"The
people
that walked
in darkness have
seen a great light."
(Isaiah 9:2).

As
they drew on the
papers that were spread
out before them, their teacher
walked up and down the rows of her
class of kindergarten children, observing
their work. She stopped at the desk of a little
girl and asked her about her composition. The
child replied, "I'm drawing a picture of God."
The teacher paused, and then hesitantly said:
"But no one knows what God looks like."
Without missing a beat or looking up
from her paper, the girl replied:
"They will in a minute."
(Anonymous).

October 13

"We are buried
with him by baptism
unto death, that like as
Christ was raised up from
the dead by the glory of
the Father, even so we
also should walk in
newness of life."
(Romans 6:4).

By being immersed in the
stream, we qualify for membership in
the Lord's church, but the ordinance does
not assure us of the spiritual transformation
that is necessary to regain the presence of God.
This comes through the baptism of fire and the
Holy Ghost, for it is "by the water (that we)
keep the commandment; by the Spirit
(that we) are justified, and by the
blood (of Christ that we) are
(ultimately) sanctified."
(Moses 6:60).

October 14

"Woe unto you,
ye blind guides."
(Matthew 23:16).

Far
too often,
we shoot the
arrow blindly, and
then hastily move the
target so that we can score
what we perceive to be a bulls-
eye. When we distort the doctrine,
we play right into the hands of Satan,
who strokes our necks with flaxen cords
until we find ourselves bound with his
strong chains. When we compromise
our core values, we strain our eyes
and lose our focus. We damage
our powers of discernment. It
then becomes all too easy
for us to look beyond
the mark.

October 15

He "washed
us from our sins
in his own blood."
(Revelation 1:5).

In
a rite
from the
dim recesses
of time that is as
all-encompassing as it is
beautiful in its simplicity, the
penitent faithful are symbolically
cleansed in the redeeming blood of the
Lamb of God as they approach His holy altar
with the sacrifice of a broken heart and contrite
spirit. They rely on the merits of Christ that rest
in the power of His Atonement, and in the first
principles and ordinances of the gospel that are
plainly taught in the scriptures. It is only thru
His magnificent love and incomprehensible
grace that they are then released from the
bondage of the insufferable weight of
responsibility to satisfy Justice by
paying for their own sins
in the absence of Him
who is both willing
and able to
do so.

October 16

"Ye cannot serve
God and mammon."
(Matthew 6:24).

We are
independent
in every stage of
development to which
our decisions have led us.
And still, when we engage our
agency within the bounds the Lord
has set, we limit our options. Our good
choices are, to some degree, the result of
our unconscious decisions not to settle for
less satisfying options. We thereby avoid
the compulsions that result from endless
re-enactments, until a point is reached
where, as William James observed:
"Unlimited freedom leads to
unlimited tyranny."

October 17

"I
am Alpha
and Omega, the
beginning and the end,
saith the Lord, which is,
and which was, and
which is to come."
(Revelation 1:8).

Is
there
anything
the Lord does
not know? He is
Alpha & Omega, the
Beginning and the
End, Whose eye
pierceth all
things.

October 18

"Is
there
no balm in
Gilead? Is there
no physician there?"
(Jeremiah 8:22).

The
question: "Who is
that Samaritan?" is asked so
contemptuously. What reasons
compel his selfless acts of charity?
He performs his works not to be seen
of men, but in secret does he follow
the Master. His motivation is pure
and without guile. Sweetly, then,
is the Savior of the world given
all of the credit, as would be
expected from any disciple
who walked in the ways
of the Lord, in the
brilliant light
of day.

October 19

"For neither at
any time use we flattering
words, as ye know, nor a
cloak of covetousness."
(1 Thessalonians 2:5).

The authority of the
priesthood may be exercised
only under the direction of the one
holding the right, which is the key to its
implementation. Its power only functions in
accord with the characteristics and attributes of
God; namely persuasion, long-suffering, gentleness,
meekness, love unfeigned, righteousness and virtue,
knowledge, justice, judgment, mercy, and truth.
It ceases to exist when it is used to obtain the
honors of the world, or to gratify pride,
to cover sin or evil, or to exercise
unrighteous dominion.

October 20

"For thou wilt light my
candle. The Lord my God
will enlighten my darkness."
(Psalms 18:28).

To the twenty six year
old Prophet Joseph Smith, the
Lord revealed an astounding truth,
when He declared: "The Spirit giveth light
to every man that cometh into the world, and the
Spirit enlighteneth every man through the world that
hearkeneth to the voice of the Spirit." (D&C 84:46). God
has endowed our minds with the ability to resonate with
recognition when they encounter truth, so that ultimately
every one who listens, as it were, to the voice of the Spirit
may eventually come unto Him. Helen Keller wondered:
"Why cannot the soul discard the poor lenses of the body
and peer through the telescope of truth into the infinite
reaches of immortality," possessed of an eternal focus
that receives its clarity from an otherworldly "light"
that stands independently and in defiance of any
rational explanation or secular apology?

October 21

"He that
soweth the
good seed is
the Son of man."
(Matthew 13:37).

Study, prayer,
and our commitment,
empower us by enlarging
our souls and enlightening our
understanding. As Brigham Young
famously said: "Every gospel principle
carries within it a witness that it is true."
From the matchless economy that is found
in heaven, "we often catch a spark from the
awakened memories of the immortal soul,
which lights up our whole being as with
the glory of our former home."
(Joseph F. Smith).

October 22

"Wheresoever the
carcass is, there will the eagles be
gathered together; so likewise shall
mine elect be gathered from the
four quarters of the earth."
(J.S. Matthew 1:27).

The gathering that has been
foretold in the scriptures is taking
place in our day, not only among the Jews
in Israel, but also among the literal and adopted
descendants of Ephraim, who have been gathering
since 1830 as members of The Church of Jesus Christ
of Latter-day Saints. They have been commissioned by
God to bring the message of salvation to a world that
is in desperate need. With priesthood authority and
by the administration of ordinances, Ephraim
will provide the nations of the earth with
the covenant blessings that have been
promised to Abraham and to
his righteous seed.

October 23

"O Jerusalem, loose thyself from the bands of thy neck, O captive daughter of Zion." (Isaiah 52:2).

It was to the gathered Saints that Joseph Smith explained: "The scattered remnants are exhorted to return to the Lord from whence they have fallen; which if they do, the promise of the Lord is that he will speak to them, or give them revelation. ...The bands of her neck are the scattered curses of God upon her, or the remnants of Israel in their scattered condition among the Gentiles." (D&C 113:10).

October 24

"Man
doth not live
by bread only,
but by every word
that proceedeth out of
the mouth of the Lord."
(Deuteronomy 8:3).

Churches that
operate on borrowed
light are sometimes quite
popular with those who seek
form without a substance, and
who enjoy the relative ease of
expending minimal effort as
members of organizations
that make precious few
demands for personal
sacrifice, or even for
random acts of
kindness.

October 25

"The
God of
my rock; in
him will I trust.
He is my shield, and
the horn of my salvation,
my high tower, and my
refuge, my savior."
(2 Samuel 22:3).

When
we sink our
roots down in
the earthy loam
of covenants and
ordinances, and the
foundations of life are
grounded in the gospel,
we find the Savior's love
and encouragement to be
just the underpinning that
we need, in order for us to
firmly establish our footings
well beneath the frost line of
faithlessness and far beyond
every conceivable limitation
to our progression, such as
selfishness, greed, pride,
immorality, and
dishonesty.

October 26

"Before
their face the
people shall be
much pained. All
faces shall gather
blackness."
(Joel 2:6).

Lord,
I prostrate
myself before
thy face, and grow
weak in Thy presence.
The Pleasing Bar of Christ
is continually before me, as
I prepare, and feel Thy love,
even as I anticipate the
dawn of a brighter
day.

October 27

"It is
written,
My house
shall be called
(a) house of prayer;
but ye have made it
a den of thieves."
(Matthew 21:13).

O Lord,
grant us a haven
from the world. At
Bethel, may we find
refuge; in the House
of God, Who is our
Rest. May we go
there and tightly
grasp the horns
of peace and
sanctuary.

October 28

"The tongue of the just
is as choice silver."
(Proverbs 10:20).

When we
speak to others with
decisiveness and with precision,
it is seen as a virtue, but without love
unfeigned it can be cruel. When we back
people into corners, the only way they can
come out is swinging. Accompanied by love,
however, candor manifests itself with a sense
of integrity that will shine as a light through
our eyes. May we always possess the virtue
to encourage those most sought-after of all
the character traits, to be known not only
for our forthrightness, but also for our
tender hearts, benevolent blindness,
and for our willingness to quickly
and unconditionally extend our
forgiveness to others for their
perceived faults and
shortcomings.

October 29

"For I
perceive that
thou art in the
gall of bitterness,
and in the bond
of iniquity."
(Acts 8:23).

Those
who have
become mired in
the bonds of iniquity
know despair very well.
It is the hopelessness they
feel when they must deal with
the sense of futility that comes
from having to choose between
alternatives that are equally
disappointing because
they are fruitless,
or devoid of
value.

October 30

"For brass, I will
bring gold, and for
iron, I will bring silver,
and for stones, iron."
(Isaiah 60:17).

The image of
a Brazen Serpent is
ever before us, and yet
we eat, drink, and make
merry in an engagement
with Spiritual Babylon.
In a dance with death,
we look beyond the
mark that is in
our midst.

October 31

"Ye are the light
of the world. A city
that is set on a hill
cannot be hid."
(Matthew 5:14).

"Let your preaching be
the warning voice, every man to
his neighbor, in mildness and meekness."
(D&C 38:41). When Spencer W. Kimball urged
members to lengthen their stride, he knew that their
spirituality would be intensified. Christ urged those
"in bondage to go the second mile, to double their
stride. The second mile is a gift of spiritual
independence that removes the veil of
insensitivity to a divine destiny."
(Richard L. Gunn).

November 1

"The
heavens
shall vanish
away like smoke,
and the earth shall
wax old like a garment,
and they that dwell therein
shall die in like manner. But my
salvation shall be forever, and
my righteousness shall
not be abolished."
(Isaiah 51:6).

When
we enter into
the presence of
God, nothing will
escape His attention,
and we will realize that
forever is now. "As time is
no more, likewise space will
shrink irrevocably. For all we
know, the speed of light may
prove to be too slow to do
what must be done."
(Neal A. Maxwell).

November 2

"Be not wise in thine
own eyes. Fear the Lord,
and depart from evil. It
shall be health to thy
navel, and marrow
to thy bones."
(Proverbs 3:7-8).

The Saints are
happiest when they
observe the summons to
gather in their sanctuaries
to enjoy the companionship
of the Spirit, where they shall
receive not only health in their
navels, but also a life sustaining
marrow in their bones; even as
their delighted congregations
reverberate with the pleasant
sounds of the anticipation of
an even more enthralling
reunification in heaven
with their Father
Who is their
God.

November 3

"The righteous need not fear.
But …all those who belong to the
kingdom of the devil are they who
need fear, and tremble, and quake;
they are those who must be brought
low in the dust; they are those who
must be consumed as stubble;
and this is according to the
words of the prophet.
(1 Nephi 22:22-23).

The Lord has given
repeated reassurance that it is His
hand that will rule in the Last Days,
and so His people need not fear the vile
threats and dreadful oaths of the wicked.
He has promised: "I will make thy horn
iron, and I will make thy hoofs brass.
And thou shalt beat in pieces many
people; and I will consecrate their
gain unto the Lord, and their
substance unto the Lord
of the whole earth."
(3 Nephi 20:19).

November 4

"We wrestle not against flesh and blood, but against principalities, against powers, against the rulers of darkness of this world, against spiritual wickedness in high places."
(Ephesians 6:12).

O, that I might possess the meekness to become an instrument in Thine hand, and as Boanerges, preach the word of truth. May I go forth as a Son of Thunder among men, and armed with Thy power, might, mind, and strength, do nothing except that which is Thy holy will.

November 5

My yoke is easy, and
my burden is light."
(Matthew 11:30).

The truth
can free us from
sin, guilt, confusion,
skepticism, apprehension,
misgiving, uncertainty, and
ignorance. It can liberate us to
make thoughtful choices, receive
priesthood ordinances, and to serve
others with more charity, influence,
and significance. As we more fully
enjoy the blessings of the Plan of
Salvation, continuing obedience
to gospel principles moves us
steadily forward along the
path that leads back to
our heavenly home
and the warm
embrace of
God.

November 6

"Behold, the days come,
saith the Lord God, that I will
send a famine in the land, not a
famine of bread, nor a thirst
for water, but of hearing
the words of the Lord."
(Amos 8:11).

We
respond to
His command to
search out wisdom,
even hidden fountains
of knowledge, as we look
in secret places in the spirit
of truth. Surely there can be
no hidden thing that shall
escape the scrutiny of
our attention in our
determination to
know and do
His will.

November 7

"His
fruit shall be a
fiery flying serpent."
(2 Nephi 24:29).

When
we neglect
to exercise our
hearts, allowing
them to harden with
spiritual sclerosis through
transgression, comprehension
of even the most basic of doctrines
may be withheld, leaving us even more
vulnerable to the influence of the devil. The
effect of sin on those who have been taught the
principles of the gospel is that the guidance of the
Spirit is withdrawn, leaving them alone as they grope
about in the darkness. Guilt causes them to shrink from
fellowship with the Saints, until they have no claim on
the blessings of prosperity or preservation. Having
ears, they hear not, and having eyes, the see not.
They are deaf to the entreaties of others, and
are as the blind leading the blind, who
put themselves at great risk of
falling into the ditches that
loom large before them
and seem to hedge
up their way.

November 8

"I have seen all the works that are done under the sun, and, behold, all is vanity and vexation of spirit."
(Ecclesiastes 1:4).

The world is increasing in narcissism, and vanity now seems pandemic. It constantly tugs at us, trying to pull us away from our divine center. We must not stray from our Father's business, but instead consecrate all that we are, including our time and talents, to promote the gospel of Jesus Christ and the cause of Zion.

November 9

"For God so loved the
world, that he gave his only
begotten Son, that whosoever
believeth in him should
not perish, but have
everlasting life."
(John 3:16).

We
are not born
born of blood, or
even of water, but
of spirit, in celestial
realms, and thus we
trace the pattern of
a nobler heritage.
We are offspring
of God, born of
royalty and
bathed in
light.

November 10

"Consider the
lilies of the field, how
they grow. They toil not,
neither do they spin. And
yet I say unto you, that
even Solomon in all his
glory was not arrayed
like one of these."
(Matthew 6:28-29).

"God has not promised
skies that will always be blue, or
flower strewn pathways all our lives
thru. Nor has He promised sun without
rain, joy without sorrow, or peace without
pain. What He has promised is strength for
the day, rest from our labors, and light for
our way; grace for our trials, help from
above, unfailing sympathy, and most
importantly, His undying love."
(Anonymous).

November 11

"Cast out first the beam out of thine own eye, and then shalt thou see clearly to pull out the mote that is in thy brother's eye."
(Luke 6:42).

The Savior employed the metaphor of the mote and the beam to illustrate that it seems to be our human nature to point out the sins of others, and to emphasize their weaknesses, though it is we who are frequently guilty of more serious transgressions.

November 12

"If he trespass against thee seven times in a day, and seven times in a day turn again to thee, saying I repent, thou shalt forgive him." (Luke 17:4).

The Lord said "I will forgive whom I will forgive, but of you it is required to forgive all men." (D&C 64:10). Not only our eternal salvation, but also our joy and our satisfaction in life, meaning our true freedom, depend on our willingness and capacity to forgive others for the perceived injustices that they have committed, that have supposedly harmed us.

November 13

"He hath
sent me to bind
up the brokenhearted,
to proclaim liberty to the
captives, and the opening
of the prison to them
that are bound."
(Isaiah 61:1).

When our hearts
have been bruised by
the painful recognition of
our sins, it is much easier to
negotiate the path to complete
repentance. Those whose hearts
are broken are softened to receive
the Spirit. They are teachable, since
their faith has wrought upon them to
convict them of their sins. As soon as
they have descended into the depths
of humility to cast themselves before
the altar of Christ, that they might
trust upon His Atonement, they
are set free from their bondage
to sin. His grace blesses them
with the unfathomable gift
of His unconditional
forgiveness.

November 14

"There was given to
me a thorn in the flesh,
the messenger of Satan to
buffet me, lest I should be
exalted above measure."
(2 Corinthians 12:7).

The
highest pinnacle
to which those who
enjoy a spiritual life may
hope to ascend is not joy in
unbroken sunshine, but absolute
and undoubting trust in the love of
God. Each of us must endure a soaking
rain now and then, together with the mud
that follows the deluge. Lest we forget, "I
Ching" is always there to remind us that
change comes as a clap of thunder and
a flash of lightning. But after the
storm, we can be certain
that flowers will
bloom.

November 15

"The
vineyard
of the Lord
of hosts is the
house of Israel;
the men of Judah..
his pleasant plant."
(Isaiah 5:7).

The
Stick of Judah
has nourished the
Gentiles as manna in
the wilderness of their
journey to Christ. While
the Stick of Joseph is a
gift to the Lamanites,
as the bread of life
to the branch that
has grown up
beyond the
wall.

November 16

"Whatsoever a
man soweth, that
shall he also reap."
(Galatians 6:7).

Since
each one of us
will be judged by the
laws to which we were
accountable throughout our
lives, our responsibility before
the Bar to explain our behavior
will differ, depending upon our
unique circumstances. However,
the gospel does not discriminate,
and each of us is alike unto God.
We enjoy the Light of Christ that
gives us the perspective to see
beyond the limited horizon
of our vision, to act upon
our promptings, and to
do what is right. At
the end of the day,
each one of us is
accountable
to God.

November 17

"The harvest truly
is plenteous, but the
labourers are few."
(Matthew 9:37).

The
humble
servants of
the Lord preach
faith and repentance.
Offering the ordinances
of baptism and the Holy Ghost,
they teach the gospel to a world that
is dying of spiritual thirst. The repentant
guilty wander across the deserts of Idumea
and Babylon. They seek the cleansing waters
of redemption, and long for the healing balm
of Gilead from saviors on Mount Zion, who
are prepared to reveal to their open hearts
the certain knowledge of the love and
concern of their Father Who
dwells in heaven.

November 18

"I will make my
words in thy mouth
fire, and this people
wood, and it shall
devour them."
(Jeremiah 5:14).

As
the white hot
sparks of faith are
struck off the divine
anvil of God, they ignite
the flames of resolve within
the Lord's disciples to expand
their power to do whatever is
right. They will kindle a fire
that will burns as a bright
beacon of faith in the
anticipation of the
return of their
true King.

November 19

"For as
the lightning
cometh out of the
east, and shineth even
unto the west; so shall
also the coming of the
Son of Man be."
(Matthew 24:27).

Our
Pilot guides us
across uncharted waters as
we sail the vast oceans of life.
He never ceases to encourage us
to continually take our bearings on
eternity. We are reassured by brightly
burning stars that are ever twinkling on a
celestial horizon. It may be at the conclusion
of a day trip, or only when our life's voyage
is over, that we come to realize that the wind
and the waves were always on the side of
the ablest Navigator, who as it turns
out, has all along been the Master
of our vessel.

November 20

The record of our lives
is "written not with ink, but
with the Spirit of the living God;
not in tables of stone, but in
fleshy tables of the heart."
(2 Corinthians 3:3).

The Torah has
been written not with
ink, nor on paper with
pen, but within our hearts,
and it unerringly guides our
actions. Without our conscious
effort, we hold securely to the rod
of iron, for we intuitively know it
to be true. God's Law has been
stitched into our sinews by
the power of the Holy
Ghost.

November 21

"He
maketh me
to lie down in
green pastures."
(Psalms 23:2).

"Sometimes,
during solitude, I hear
truth spoken with clarity
and freshness. Uncolored and
untranslated, it speak from within
myself in a language original but
inarticulate, heard only with the
soul, and I realize I brought it
with me, was never taught
it, nor can I efficiently
teach it to another."
(Hugh B. Brown).

November 22

"And thou
shalt make... an
holy anointing oil."
(Exodus 30:25).

That
man who loves
both his wife and his
children will consecrate
his behavior to secure the
blessings and benedictions
of celestial glories. He will
be rewarded to reign as a
king and as a priest. He
will become the leader
of a dominion whose
reach is bound only
by the holy Order
of the Son of
God.

November 23

"Except a man
be born of water
and of the Spirit, he
cannot enter into the
kingdom of God."
(John 3:5).

When
just eight
years old, our
children receive the
ordinance of baptism
and enter in at the strait
gate. The way is narrowly
defined and invites our little
ones to be immersed as soon
as they have arrived at that
age of accountability, and
then to receive the gift of
the Holy Ghost. For it is
by both water and the
Spirit that they are
sanctified to
enjoy His
gifts.

November 24

"Cast thy
bread upon
the waters, for
thou shalt find it
after many days."
(Ecclesiastes 11:1).

Happiness is
like a butterfly. The
more you chase it, the
more it eludes you. But
if you turn your attention
to selfless acts and service
in behalf of others, it will
come and rest quietly
on your shoulder.
(Anonymous).

November 25

"Said
the Lord
unto Moses:
Behold, I will
rain bread from
heaven for you."
(Exodus 16:4).

Send
not a famine
into the land, but
grant instead that we
may live in Bethlehem.
For Thy habitation is
as a house of bread,
where the faithful
go to partake of
Thy word that
is the true
staff of
life.

November 26

"I...created the heavens
and the earth."
(D&C 14:9).

God
pronounced
all things good,
and even very good,
that He had made at the
creation. Then He gave it
into our care, to be dressed,
nurtured, and protected. But it
remains His handiwork, and the
earth, together with all its flora and
fauna, is His footstool, and not ours to
be used according to our whim. Ours is
a sacred trust, and the manner in which
we carry out our stewardship is not
open to discussion, argument,
or interpretation.

November 27

"Let your light so
shine before men, that they
may see your good works,
and glorify your Father
which is in heaven."
(Matthew 5:16).

The Saints of
the Most High God are
as lights unto the world. They
are as beacons to those seeking the
truth, and saviors on Mount Zion to
both the living and the dead. They
are as missionary companions to
the Author of salvation, Who
embedded its principles
within His gospel
Plan.

November 28

"Blessed are they which are called unto the marriage supper of the Lamb."
(Revelation 19:9).

Every family that has been created by the power and authority of God becomes another of eternity's basic building blocks. The Church of Jesus Christ emphasizes the worth of the family and holds it in the highest esteem. It regards the family as a definitive expression of both individuality and creativity. But more than that, it is a tangible reflection of the glory of God.
(See Moses 1:39).

November 29

"I will
not put my trust
in the arm of flesh."
(2 Nephi 4:34).

The first principle of
the gospel is faith. Therefore,
profane temporal power is a curse to
those who put their trust in its ephemeral
authority. For the support of the devil and his
angels will be a millstone around the necks of
the heart-hearted and stiff-necked at the last
day, when they will be abandoned and left
terrifyingly alone, as they are catapulted,
kicking and screaming, down into an
abyss of their own creation, that is
their very own hand-crafted,
personalized version
of hell.

November 30

"In my Father's house
are many mansions."
(John 14:2).

Sinai
is an attitude,
and is not a place.
The faithful loose the
latchets of their shoes
when they see bushes
that burn, but that are
not consumed. Holy
sanctuaries, as we
begin to realize,
can be our own
personalized
versions of
His Rest.

December 1

"He
shall baptize you
with the Holy Ghost,
and with fire."
(Matthew 3:11).

As a
present, in
commemoration of
the occasion of our being
born again, every member of the
church "is given a gift by the Spirit of
God." (D&C 46:11). These gifts are positive,
motivational, uplifting, and enduring. In the
fiery crucible that is the learning laboratory of
life, it is our spiritual gifts that provide us with
repetitive opportunities to vividly role-play,
with the Holy Ghost acting as our dialogue
coach. For our life lessons to be helpful,
we must pre-play and then re-play,
and we must practice over and
over again until we get it
right, even so that we
can do it with our
eyes closed.

December 2

"Upon this rock I will
build my church, and the
gates of hell shall not
prevail against it."
(Matthew 16:18).

Gleaming
jaws epitomize
the gateway to hell.
They are dripping with a
sickening slurry of the saliva
of Satan that has been saturated
with sin. They menacingly portray
the entrance to the forbidding spirit
prison of the unjust. The way to avoid
this awful portal is to offer the Lord the
required sacrifice, which is to be broken
in our hearts with sorrow for sin, and
in the spirit of contrition to come to
Him in an attitude of sincere and
purposeful repentance, that we
might obtain forgiveness
through His tender
mercies.

December 3

"The
beloved of the
Lord shall dwell
in safety by him, and
the Lord shall cover him
all the day long, and he shall
dwell between his shoulders."
(Deuteronomy 33:12).

When
we have been
enveloped within the
tender watch care of the
Lord, we begin to enjoy the
glimmering facets of the light of
the Spirit. With enhanced vision, we
see as clearly as did Hans Christian
Anderson. We know that every one
of our lives can be as a fairy tale
"waiting to be written by the
finger of God."

December 4

"I
bring
near my
righteousness.
It shall not be far
off, and my salvation
shall not tarry; and I will
place salvation in Zion
for Israel my glory."
(Isaiah 46:13).

The substance
of the gospel is not so
much the sum of "Thou shalt
not" commandments, as it is "Thou
shalt" commandments. Their composite
principles are the consummate compilation
of affirmative actions. When we are converted
to Zion's lifestyle, the relationship between the
commandments and blessings becomes blurred.
Our obedience forges an unbreakable bond with
God and His bounty. It is in the covenants of
the holy priesthood that the real power of
godliness is manifest. Without them, we
could never muster confidence in the
One who is standing at the helm
to help us negotiate dangerous
currents and navigate thru
treacherous shoals on
the vast ocean
of life.

December 5

"Live together in love, insomuch that thou shalt weep for the loss of them that die, and more especially for those that have not hope of a glorious resurrection."
(D&C 42:45).

The philosopher observed: When you came into this world, you cried and others rejoiced. When you leave it, others will cry, and you will rejoice.

December 6

"For
they have
sown the wind,
and they shall reap
the whirlwind."
(Hosea 8:7).

When
we are in the
midst of conflict, let us
remember that "the mystic
chords of memory, stretching
from every battlefield and patriot
grave to every living heart and hearth
stone all over this broad land, will yet
again swell the chorus of (our) Union
when again touched, as surely they
will be, by the better angels of our
nature." (Abraham Lincoln).

December 7

"He
healeth
the broken in
heart, and bindeth
up their wounds."
(Psalms 147:3).

The
Spirit
works on
us to break us
down with a deep
sorrow for our sins, so
that we become humble
and thoroughly penitent.
Only then will His atoning
sacrifice have the power
to bind up our wounds
and heal all of our
infirmities.

December 8

"They that be whole
need not a physician,
but they that are sick."
(Matthew 9:12).

It is at the
very instant when our
unsatisfied desire for the praise
and popularity of the world begins
to control our actions, that we will find
ourselves in the uncomfortable position of
bending our character, when we think we
are only taking a bow. It is especially at
these times that we need the softening
guidance of the Spirit, and then the
healing influence of our Lord and
Savior Jesus Christ, and finally
the loving encouragement
of our Father, Who looks
down upon us, every
day of our lives,
from heaven
above.

December 9

"Let
your loins be
girded about, and
your lights burning."
(Luke 12:35).

By its very
own description and
definition, it is the gospel of
Jesus Christ that encourages us to
be enthusiastic. After all, it is the good
news. It practically begs us to experience
the feeling of being possessed by a god, to
have supernatural inspiration, and even a
prophetic frenzy. The definition found
in the dictionary is unmistakable. If
we are charged with enthusiasm,
our actions are no longer ours;
for it is God Who has taken
control of our destiny
with kindness and
benevolence.

December 10

"No
weapon that
is formed against
thee shall prosper, and
every tongue that shall rise
against thee in judgment,
thou shalt condemn."
(Isaiah 54:17).

I
will delight
in the Savior's
commandments.
They are a blessing
to the faithful. He will
prosper all those who
trust Him, who love
Him, and who
abide by His
words.

December 11

"Be ye clean that bear the
vessels of the Lord."
(Isaiah 52:11).

I
shall
not fail
to warn my
neighbors, or
neglect to fulfill
the commandments
of the Lord. With all of
my heart and as I receive
inspiration from the Spirit
I will teach the gospel, by
precept, and by example,
and by my voice, with
gentleness, and with
love unfeigned.

December 12

"The
mountain was
full of horses and
chariots of fire round
about Elisha."
(2 Kings 6:17).

Of Whom shall I
sing, and to Whom do
I find myself compelled to
shout hosanna? To the Lord
of Hosts, my Redeemer. He is
my Shelter, my Refuge, and
my Sanctuary. My Savior
is Jehovah. Surely God
will save now, and I
shall praise Him
forevermore,
before His
throne.

December 13

"To him
that overcometh
will I grant to sit with
me in my throne."
(Revelation 3:21).

Brigham Young was
once asked if he knew where
we are going when we lay down
our tabernacle of flesh. He replied:
"Into the spirit world." Then he asked
rhetorically: "Where is the spirit world?"
"It is right here," he responded. "Do the
spirits go beyond the boundaries of this
organized earth?" he continued. "No,
they do not. They can see us, but
we cannot see them, unless our
eyes have been opened"
to the limitless vista
of spiritual
reality.

December 14

Write the
commandments
"upon the table of
thine heart."
(Proverbs 7:3).

Our
priesthood
leaders prick our
hearts with the word,
continually stirring us up
to purposeful repentance.
Their responsibility, thru
the power and authority
of God, is to heal us of
our deafness and our
blindness, and at the
same time apply the
curative balm that
is needed for our
aching spiritual
muscles and
joints.

December 15

"Ye
have taken
away the key
of knowledge."
(Luke 11:52).

The Spirit of God
extends to each of us the
invitation to receive revelation.
Upon our acceptance, our Father
in Heaven blesses us with both light
and knowledge. "No matter what ability
and talent we may possess, all must come
under this rule if they wish to know the
Father and the Son. If knowledge of
them is not obtained through
revelation, it cannot be
obtained at all."
(John Taylor).

December 16

"The
desolation
of abominations
awaits the wicked."
(D&C 88:85).

Wickedness is
the close companion of
frailty, friability, and futility.
It is the bedfellow of despondency,
desperation and distress. Those poor
lost souls who abound in iniquity have
no hope of progression, forgiveness,
redemption, or salvation. Without
hope, they must despair; for
spiritual death is the
wages of sin. (See
Romans 6:23)

December 17

"I am
the way, the
truth, and the life."
(John 14:6).

A
grasp
of the truth
is the first critical
step that must be taken
before we can hope to reach
a successful conclusion to any
intellectual or spiritual journey,
but this is especially so, if our desire is
to obtain mercy before the Bar of Judgment.
Truth is deed, and our belief is that catalyzing
influence that motivates us to purposeful action.
The horizon of our knowledge extends only as far
as our action. This is why deeds are an important
companion to vital, active faith. Faith without
works has no life-generating or sustaining
power, because alone, it is vain; it is
impotent, ineffective, and is
inadequate to the task
at hand.

December 18

"The Lord
hath broken the
staff of the wicked,
and the sceptre
of the rulers."
(Isaiah 14:5).

Although
the adversary of
all that is good continues
to sorely tempt me , yet will
I cry unto the Lord, for He has
spoken by the mouth of His holy
prophets that I should seek Him
with all my heart, might, mind,
and strength. I will find Him,
and He will yet deliver my
soul from the gaping jaws
of death that patiently
lie in wait before
me, hoping to
snap shut
on my
soul.

December 19

"As ye have
therefore received
Christ Jesus the Lord,
so walk ye in him."
(Colossians 2:6).

In the middle years
of the nineteenth century,
the Russian novelist Leo Tolstoy
became familiar with the teachings
of the church. He was thereafter moved
to declare: "If Mormonism could be true
to its foundations and remain unchanged for
four generations, it might well become the most
powerful social influence in the world." While
we still wait for that to happen, it is becoming
a distinct possibility. The church remains a
bastion of stability and a beacon of hope
in a world that is, by all reasonable
accounts, rapidly coming apart at
the seams in chaos, confusion,
and depravity, with no
end to the freefall
in sight.

December 20

"There
are celestial bodies,
and bodies terrestrial, but
the glory of the celestial is
one, and the gory of the
terrestrial is another."
(1 Corinthians 15:40).

When we
have been blessed
by the Spirit to "tingle
with the consciousness of
our kinship with the infinite,
all the petty trials, sorrows, and
sufferings of this life will fade away
as temporary, harmless visions,
seen (only) in a dream."
(David O. McKay).

December 21

"The words
of the Lord are
pure words, as sliver
tried in a furnace of earth,
purified seven times."
(Psalms 12:6).

I
will
determine
to search the
scriptures daily. In
the face of competing
activities, I will persevere.
Although there will surely be
many influences that attempt
to weaken my resolve, yet I
will continually turn my
face to the word of
the Lord.

December 22

"To
whom is
the arm of the
Lord revealed?"
(Isaiah 53:1).

When the
arm of the Lord has
been revealed, we can
be certain of His mighty
power; our sure source of
strength and support. The
arm of flesh, conversely,
is unstable, and is prone
to uncontrollable spasm,
atrophy, and paralysis,
that are all symptoms
of clumsy outbursts
of behavior that is
destructive and
ineffectual.

December 23

"Will ye not
now return unto me,
and repent of your sins,
and be converted, that
I may heal you?"
(3 Nephi 9:13).

Thou
art mighty
to save! Forgive
all those who walk
in darkness, and who
know not where to find
gospel truth. Our hearts
reach out to those who
helplessly endure the
night and suffer the
pain of spiritual
blindness.

December 24

"Christ was once
offered to bear the sins
of many; and unto them that
look for him shall he appear
the second time without
sin unto salvation."
(Hebrews 9:28).

My
salvation is
of the Lord and
He will not fail me.
He will not deny me
His Spirit, for He is
not only my Rock,
but He is also my
Savior and my
Redeemer.
(Jonah 2:9).

December 25

"They that be
wise shall shine as the
brightness of the firmament,
and they that turn many to
righteousness as the stars
forever and ever."
(Daniel 12:3).

"If the
stars in heaven
should appear but one
night in a thousand years, how
would men believe and adore, and
preserve for many generations, the
remembrance of the city of God
which had been revealed."
(Ralph Waldo Emerson).

December 26

"And one
shall say unto him:
What are these wounds
in thine hands?"
(Zechariah 13:6).

In
the last days
on God's earth,
we cry "hallelujah!"
Before the millennial
day, when the signs of
the times proclaim that
the Second Coming of
Jesus Christ is nigh at
hand, the faithful
and true will cry:
Praise ye the
Lord!

December 27

"Our God is
a consuming fire."
(Hebrews 12:29).

A
dancing fire,
billowing clouds
of smoke, as well as
an ethereal light, a sharp
and penetrating spirit, and
deeply penetrating burnings,
are all symbolic of the presence
of the Lord and of the glory of
God, and frequently depict
the splendor of celestial
realms. In the words of
Joseph Smith: "God
Himself dwells
in eternal
fire."

December 28

"The Lord
is my shepherd;
I shall not want."
(Psalm 23:1).

O Lord,
promise to care
for me in Bethesda,
when I come to Thee in
great need. For I carry
heavy burdens, as I
seek a tabernacle
of mercy and
a house of
grace.

December 29

"The tares
are the children
of the wicked one."
(Matthew 13:38).

In the Lord's
familiar parable, healthy
stalks of wheat bore a striking
resemblance to young and tender
tares, whose benign appearance was
both succulent and fresh, but whose
supposed innocence was disarming.
Their attractive façade was, in truth,
a beguiling invitation to partake,
for it was a poisonous gift that
awaited the unwary. It was
only as the plants began
to mature, that their
deceit became
deadly.

December 30

"By their fruits,
ye shall know them."
(Matthew 7:20).

"Truth,
as well as error,
may be recognized by
its effects. The claims of the
gospel may be tested by rendering
obedience to their principles of action.
Practicing our religion is the most
direct method of gaining a
testimony of the truth."
(John Widtsoe).

December 31

"And he
shall be called Jesus
Christ, the Son of God, the
Father of heaven and earth,
the Creator of all things
from the beginning."
(Mosiah 3:8).

We have a
mutually nurturing
relationship with God as
we help Him to bring to pass our
immortality and eternal life within
the biological broth whose secret spice is
unbridled free will. It is unthinkable that He
would focus His energies and concentrate His
powers on an activity that was doomed to failure
because of flaws in the instruments that are not only
critical to its success but are also the very center of His
attention. The little boy's exclamation that "God don't
make junk!" betrays a keen wisdom beyond his years.
It may be that Victor Hugo also heard the majestic
clockwork when he wrote: "Be like a bird that
pausing in her flight a while on boughs to
light, feels them give way beneath her
and yet sings, knowing that
she has wings."

Author's Note

As you peruse the pages of this book, you will recognize that it is really nothing more than a calendar with commentary corresponding to each of 366 scriptures that loosely utilize symbols to emphasize their meaning. I wanted to provide at least a full year's worth of thoughts, which in hindsight may have been an ambitious and unrealistic goal. I leave for you, dear reader, to do with these entries what you will. As for me, I can breathe a deep sigh of relief that this endeavor is over, and move on to other writing projects!

You will quickly see that the thoughts that are expressed on each page have been carefully crafted to represent a variety of geometrical designs. It may be surprising to learn that the construction of these patterns has helped me to coherently organize my thoughts. In many cases, the outcome almost seems to have been foreordained, as I moved words around until, as if my magic, they dropped into their proper positions on the page.

Often, I envisioned beforehand the particular framework that I wanted to achieve, and when I had appropriately arranged the words, one or two would stand out and grab my attention, because they still didn't feel quite right. Frequently, it was not difficult to find an alternative that would not only fit better physically, but also was etymologically better suited to the spiritual concept I wished to convey. As my work on the project continued, I was intrigued by the natural evolution of the process. That made me consider whether my success might have been stimulated by unconventional thought processes, that are more commonly characterized as inspiration or discernment.

The various shapes and sizes of the expressions on each page reminded me of what vibrant colors must look like to a dog. As I pondered the geometry of the designs that were spread out before me, I realized that they might be manifestations of non-linear thinking in a cynical world that is largely governed by conventional wisdom. Maybe my idiosyncratic ramblings were just an exhibition of thought that had taken me down a different path. Maybe I wasn't crazy, or delusional, after all. Perhaps I had been simply touched by the Spirit.

We will describe non-linear thinking shortly, and in greater detail, but in the meantime, let me tease you with this possibility. Maybe Joseph Smith was one of the first non-linear thinkers. His unconventional view of the world helps to explain why he would look back on his life, and muse: "I stood alone, an unlearned youth, to combat the worldly wisdom and multiplied ignorance of eighteen centuries, with a new revelation, which...would open the eyes of more than eight hundred millions of people, and make plain the old paths." (H.C. 6:74). Or: "When we understand the character of God, He begins to unfold the heavens to us, and to tell us all about it. When we are ready to come to Him, He is ready to come to us." (H.C. 6:308). Or, "It is my meditation all the day, and more than my meat and drink, to know how I shall make the Saints of God comprehend the visions that roll like an overflowing surge before my mind. Oh! How I would delight to bring before you things which you never thought of." (H.C. 5:362). Or, "The best way to obtain truth and wisdom is not to ask it from books, but to go to God in prayer, and obtain divine teaching." ("Teachings," p. 191).

Now let us turn to linear thinking, that has been defined as "a process of thought following known cycles or step-by-step progression, where a response to a step must be elicited before another step is taken." This is the conventional way most of us think, most of the time, and in most situations it actually works quite well. However, there is always the danger of relying too heavily on the sheer logic of linear thinking, for once we have settled upon a starting point in our inquiry, there are only a limited number of avenues that lead to logical conclusions. Additionally, there is no guarantee that our starting point relies on truth, or on what I would call eternally valid principles. If we are lucky, and it does, we are certainly going to be much better off than if we had chosen a starting point that was either blatantly false, or that was so narrowly defined that it would limit our exposure to the rich variety of alternatives that might just be the best ones to provide the answers to our inquiry. In any event, we risk being led astray right from the beginning, and then finding ourselves in unfamiliar, indefensible territory from which there is no easy avenue of escape. Linear thinking is dangerous when it takes us down the road of expediency that leads to ethical and moral dilemmas, and to conundrums that can be of cosmic proportions.

Non-linear thinking, as opposed to linear thinking, is a relatively new term, which means that there is a lot of obfuscation going on when attempting to articulate its definition. But, for the sake of simplicity, let's describe it as human thought that is characterized by cerebral expansion in multiple spatial and even temporal directions, rather than in just one pre-determined linear direction. It is based on the concept that there exist multiple starting points from which the basic principles of logical thought may be applied to a problem. Consider, once again, my characterization of Joseph Smith as the quintessential non-linear thinker of the nineteenth century.

We do not have to stretch our minds very much to be immediately struck with the realization that God Himself must be the quintessential non-linear thinker, that the Plan of Salvation is its best expression, and that it might be consistent with His design to view the gospel through the clarifying lens of similar unconventional thought processes.

Non-linear thinking is expansive, and it lets creative juices run wild precisely because it is not dependent upon a self-limiting structure. It increases the sheer number of possible outcomes because it encourages multiple starting points for any endeavor. There is enough room in the world for an infinite number of non-linear thinkers, which allows us to segue right into the basic premises of the Plan of Salvation. The Plan, too, is flexible enough to accommodate those of every persuasion and inclination, for God "inviteth them all to come unto him and partake of his goodness; and he denieth none that come unto him, black and white, bond and free, male and female; and he remembereth the heathen; and all are alike unto God, both Jew and Gentile." (2 Nephi 26:33).

Non-linear thinkers who happen to be lucky enough to consciously appreciate the elasticity of the Plan of Salvation have flexible testimonies. To them, the veil is almost transparent. They are spiritually sensitive and prepared to act. As their powers expand, they experience the glittering facets of the life of the Spirit. They find themselves cast off into a stream of revelation, as if they were being carried along in the quickening currents of direct experience with God. Non-linear thinking sets them free to be creative, and sets them creative, that they might be free. In a sense, we all enter this world as non-linear thinkers. We are "born free," as it were. If that is true, from the very beginning, the stage is set for the inauguration of the perfect law of liberty. We are nurtured from our birth to master the ability to generate higher-level non-linear thought processes, that the quiet spiritual stirrings that underlie our experience might be amplified, and become the very catalyst we need to propel us into the presence of God.

Non-linear thinkers have no privileged frames of reference, which opens up almost unlimited options for them. They jump around, forward and backward, and side to side, when working through a problem. They literally see the big picture, as they move from one point on the canvas of life to another, focusing with greater sensitivity on areas that have caught their attention. This sounds a lot like how we envision that God must govern His creations.

Think of a linear slide show, contrasted with the comprehension of a huge canvas that illustrates the entire story, not from start to finish, but all at once, the beginning and the end at one and the same time, with the additional capacity to zoom in and out, to fast forward, reverse, and freeze frame. If you can visualize that, you can see why God must be a non-linear thinker. With a little practice, we can be, too.

In the thoughts expressed in this book, I hope that I have employed the best techniques of both liner and non-linear thinking, because I believe that ultimately, both are useful and important cognitive devices to be mastered. Non-linear thinking, however, is at its best when we re-examine our potential starting points, because doing that increases the possibility of selecting the right option from all the alternatives available. But somewhere during the process of inquiry, after that critical starting point has been fixed in our crosshairs, we might also want to employ linear thinking because of its efficient logic-based reasoning. Once we have embarked upon the journey, linear thinking might help us to get to the finish line in a more timely manner. How effectively we use both devices depends upon how thoroughly we have read the play book, how vigorously we exercise our gift of free will along the way, and how often we rely upon powers greater than ourselves to make necessary course corrections, in order to re-align ourselves with our envisioned goals and recalibrate our efforts to achieve them.

As you read the entries in this book, look for examples of both linear and non-linear thinking, and decide for yourself how to best incorporate them into your own style of inquiry.

Appendix

List of scriptures in chronological order,
correlated with month and date
for easy reference.

Old Testament

- Genesis 2:7 – July 3
- Genesis 2:17 – January 23
- Genesis 3:3 – June 6
- Genesis 3:22-24 - March 13
- Genesis 9:13 – September 28
- Genesis 12:7 – May 18
- Genesis 13:24 – February 11
- Genesis 19:26 – March 26
- Genesis 28:17 – July 26
- Genesis 49:22 - September 14
- Exodus 3:2 – January 28
- Exodus 12:5 – July 18
- Exodus 12:11 – January 2
- Exodus 13:21 – January 16

- Exodus 16:4 – November 25
- Exodus 17:6 – July 27
- Exodus 19:5 – June 26
- Exodus 25:6 – September 29
- Exodus 28:30 – February 16
- Exodus 30:25 – November 22
- Exodus 31:18 – September 2
- Numbers 21:9 – July 10
- Deuteronomy 8:3 – October 24
- Deuteronomy 24:1 – April 26
- Deuteronomy 26:9 – January 22
- Deuteronomy 28:23 – September 11
- Deuteronomy 28:24 – January 4
- Deuteronomy 30:19 – February 3
- Deuteronomy 31:5 – October 6
- Deuteronomy 32:8 - January 10
- Deuteronomy 32:41 – October 11
- Deuteronomy 33:12 – December 3
- 1 Samuel 10:1 – September 27
- 1 Samuel 17:45 – February 2
- 2 Samuel 22:3 – October 25
- 2 Kings 6:17 – December 12
- 1 Chronicles 16:23 – July 22
- 1 Chronicles 19:3 – August 12
- Job 12:25 – July 19
- Job 26:11 – March 25
- Psalms 2:7 – April 25
- Psalms 2:9 – April 12
- Psalms 12:6 – December 21
- Psalms 18:28 – October 20
- Psalms 19:1 – February 23
- Psalms 20:5 – October 3
- Psalms 20:7 – September 24
- Psalms 23:1 – December 28
- Psalms 23:2 – May 22
- Psalms 23:2 – November 22
- Palms 23:3 – June 29
- Psalms 23:4 – May 12

- Psalms 23:5 – April 27
- Psalms 34:18 - August 16
- Psalms 45:7 – January 9
- Psalms 51:7 – May 25
- Psalms 78:49 – October 5
- Psalms 84:11 – April 16
- Psalms 85:11 – July 24
- Psalms 118:16 - July 31
- Psalms 127:1 – April 6
- Psalms 127:4-5 – September 18
- Psalms 142:7 – June 24
- Psalms 147:3 – December 7
- Proverbs 3:7-8 – November 2
- Proverbs 7:3 – December 14
- Proverbs 7:2 – September 30
- Proverbs 10:20 – October 28
- Proverbs 11:29 - June 22
- Proverbs 20:27 – April 29
- Proverbs 24:10 - July 28
- Ecclesiastes 1:4 – November 8
- Ecclesiastes 9:11 – June 27
- Ecclesiastes 11:1 - November 24
- Ecclesiastes 12:7 – August 20
- Isaiah 1:6 – June 7
- Isaiah 1:18 – April 13
- Isaiah 2:2 – June 21
- Isaiah 2:4 – April 10
- Isaiah 5:7 – November 15
- Isaiah 5:24 – February 13
- Isaiah 5:26 – July 2
- Isaiah 6:1-2 – July 14
- Isaiah 6:8 – September 6
- Isaiah 9:2 – October 12
- Isaiah 9:6 – September 5
- Isaiah 11:4 – May 5
- Isaiah 11:5 – April 3
- Isaiah 11:6 - June 13
- Isaiah 11:7 – February 18

- Isaiah 11:9 – February 4
- Isaiah 14:5 – December 18
- Isaiah 14:8 – March 2
- Isaiah 25:4 – January 7
- Isaiah 28:16 – June 20
- Isaiah 29:9 – August 23
- Isaiah 29:10 – June 5
- Isaiah 29:18 – July 7
- Isaiah 35:1 – June 28
- Isaiah 35:6 – July 30
- Isaiah 46:13 – December 4
- Isaiah 48:1 – June 18
- Isaiah 48:4 – September 12
- Isaiah 49:2 – January 5
- Isaiah 49:25 – March 5
- Isaiah 51:3 – February 17
- Isaiah 51:6- November 1
- Isaiah 51:16 – July 4
- Isaiah 51:17 – August 24
- Isaiah 52:2 – October 23
- Isaiah 52:10 – May 1
- Isaiah 52:11 - December 11
- Isaiah 53:1 – December 22
- Isaiah 53:5 – June 11
- Isaiah 54:2 – March 16
- Isaiah 54:7 – October 4
- Isaiah 54:17 – December 10
- Isaiah 58:1 – January 13
- Isaiah 58:11 – May 19
- Isaiah 60:17 – October 30
- Isaiah 61:1 – November 13
- Isaiah 63:3 – August 26
- Isaiah 64:8 – August 18
- Isaiah 66:13 – May 26
- Isaiah 66:16 – June 4
- Isaiah 66:22 – April 15
- Jeremiah 5:14 - November 18
- Jeremiah 6:27 – January 26

- Jeremiah 8:22 – October 18
- Jeremiah 18:6 – July 25
- Jeremiah 31:29 – February 22
- Jeremiah 31:33 – May 13
- Ezekiel 28:13 – February 10
- Ezekiel 37:16 – March 4
- Daniel 12:3 – December 25
- Hosea 8:7 – December 6
- Joel 1:5 – August 9
- Joel 2:6 – October 26
- Joel 3:9-10 – February 25
- Amos 8:11 – November 6
- Zechariah 13:6 – December 26
- Malachi 3:2 – January 1
- Malachi 3:10 – May 27
- Malachi 3:16 – August 7
- Malachi 4:1 – April 2

New Testament

- Matthew 3:10 – April 8
- Matthew 3:11 - December 1
- Matthew 3:16 – August 28
- Matthew 5:5 – April 19
- Matthew 5:13 – May 3
- Matthew 5:14 – October 31
- Matthew 5:16 – November 27
- Matthew 5:18 – March 24
- Matthew 5:26 – August 30
- Matthew 5:39 – August 27
- Matthew 5:41 – March 7
- Matthew 5:45 – July 29
- Matthew 6:12 – April 21
- Matthew 6:20 – April 20
- Matthew 6:21 – February 20
- Matthew 6:22 – March 10
- Matthew 6:24 – October 16
- Matthew 6:28-29 – November 10

- Matthew 7:3 – August 1
- Matthew 7:6 – February 26
- Matthew 7:13 – January 25
- Matthew 7:15 – June 8
- Matthew 7:20 – December 30
- Matthew 7:24 – July 15
- Matthew 7:27 – September 26
- Matthew 9:12 – December 8
- Matthew 9:37 – November 17
- Matthew 10:14 – May 23
- Matthew 10:16 – June 17
- Matthew 10:30 – March 17
- Matthew 10:34 – April 17
- Matthew 10:39 – March 8
- Matthew 11:21 – May 7
- Matthew 11:25 – March 30
- Matthew 11:28 – April 30
- Matthew 11:30 – November 5
- Matthew 12:8 – May 15
- Matthew 12:25 – May 30
- Matthew 12:30 – July 9
- Matthew 12:36-37 – February 14
- Matthew 12:39 – June 9
- Matthew 12:48-50 – March 21
- Matthew 13:5-8 – August 22
- Matthew 13:15 – June 12
- Matthew 13:37 – October 21
- Matthew 13:38 – March 29
- Matthew 13:38 – May 24
- Matthew 13:38 – December 29
- Matthew 13:44 – February 19
- Matthew 13:45-46 – January 24
- Matthew 16:18 – December 2
- Matthew 21:13 – October 27
- Matthew 23:16 – October 14
- Matthew 24:27 – November 19
- Matthew 24:28 – September 21
- Matthew 27:23 – July 16

- Matthew 27:51 – April 28
- Mark 10:21 – July 23
- Luke 6:42 – November 11
- Luke 11:52 – December 15
- Luke 12:35 – December 9
- Luke 17:4 – November 12
- Luke 22:44 - January 20
- Luke 24:32 – August 10
- John 1:1 – May 11
- John 1:18 – September 17
- John 3:3 – September 25
- John 3:5 – November 23
- John 3:16 – November 9
- John 4:10 – March 23
- John 4:35 – March 18
- John 5:39 – February 8
- John 6:27 – April 7
- John 8:31-32 – July 13
- John 8:34 – July 21
- John 8:44 – June 1
- John 10:16 – May 10
- John 10:30 - June 23
- John 12:40 – February 21
- John 14:2 – November 30
- John 14:6 – December 17
- Acts 2:2 – April 1
- Acts 2:19 - February 5
- Acts 2:29 – June 27
- Acts 8:23 – October 29
- Acts 9:18 – March 15
- Acts 20:29 – June 19
- Acts 22:16 – September 8
- Romans 1:21 – February 24
- Romans 6:4 - October 13
- Romans 6:23 – April 12
- Romans 11:16 – January 15
- Romans 16:20 - September 9
- 1 Corinthians 1:17 – August 21

- 1 Corinthians 3:2 – April 23
- 1 Corinthians 3:9 – October 7
- 1 Corinthians 10: 1 & 4 – March 1
- 1 Corinthians 15:40 – December 20
- 1 Corinthians 15:51-52 – May 17
- 1 Corinthians 15:55 – May 28
- 2 Corinthians 3:3 – November 20
- 2 Corinthians 6:14 – July 1
- 2 Corinthians 7:1 – April 24
- 2 Corinthians 12:7 – November 14
- Galatians 3:24 – July 17
- Galatians 6:7 – November 16
- Ephesians 2:12 – February 12
- Ephesians 2:20 – April 11
- Ephesians 6:12 – November 4
- Ephesians 6:13 – September 20
- Ephesians 6:14 – March 19
- Ephesians 6:15 – June 15
- Colossians 2:6 – December 19
- 1 Thessalonians 2:5 – October 19
- 1 Thessalonians 5:2 – May 29
- 1 Thessalonians 5:8 – August 14
- 2 Thessalonians 2:3 - January 30
- 2 Timothy 4:8 – April 14
- Titus 1:16 – February 6
- Hebrews 4:1 – May 14
- Hebrews 4:12 – July 8
- Hebrews 9:28 – December 24
- Hebrews 12:3 – August 13
- Hebrews 12:29 – December 27
- James 1:8 – August 4
- James 1:12 – August 17
- James 5:3 – September 1
- 1 Peter 5:4 – August 8
- 2 Peter 1:19 – February 9
- 2 Peter 2:4 – February 7
- 2 Peter 2:17 – June 25
- 2 Peter 2:20 – May 21

- 1 John 2:18 – September 10
- Jude 1:6 – January 6
- Jude 1:13 – March 12
- Revelation 1:5 – October 15
- Revelation 1:8 – October 17
- Revelation 1:16 – February 28
- Revelation 2:17 – October 10
- Revelation 3:5 – August 31
- Revelation 3:9 – June 30
- Revelation 3:15 – August 15
- Revelation 3:21 – December 13
- Revelation 4:5 – May 31
- Revelation 4:6 – February 29
- Revelation 5:1 – January 18
- Revelation 12:7-8 – January 8
- Revelation 14:6 – August 3
- Revelation 14:10 – September 3
- Revelation 14:10 – August 2
- Revelation 17:2 – April 18
- Revelation 18:2 – October 2
- Revelation 18:8 – August 6
- Revelation 19:9 – November 28
- Revelation 20:1 – January 19
- Revelation 20:2 – September 13
- Revelation 20:12 – March 20

Book of Mormon

- 1 Nephi 8:23 – May 4
- 1 Nephi 8:26 - September 4
- 1 Nephi 12:17 – February 15
- 1 Nephi 13:6 – March 22
- 1 Nephi 14:10 – January 21
- 1 Nephi 16:10 – August 5
- 1 Nephi 22:9 – January 11
- 1 Nephi 22:22-23 – November 3
- 2 Nephi 4:27 – May 2
- 2 Nephi 4:33 – March 6

- 2 Nephi 4:33 – April 22
- 2 Nephi 4:34 – November 29
- 2 Nephi 9:14 – February 1
- 2 Nephi 24:29 – November 7
- 2 Nephi 26:22 – September 23
- 2 Nephi 27:27 – July 12
- 2 Nephi 27:29 - October 8
- 2 Nephi 32:3 – September 22
- Jacob 3:11 – June 3
- Jacob 5:64 – August 29
- Jarom 1:4 – March 11
- Mosiah 3:8 – December 31
- Mosiah 24:15 - July 6
- Alma 4:6 – May 16
- Alma 5:21 – May 20
- Alma 5:60 – January 17
- Alma 8:31 – June 14
- Alma 12:6 – January 31
- Alma 12:11 – January 3
- Alma 12:16 - January 14
- Alma 13:12 - October 1
- Alma 22:15 – August 25
- Alma 34:33 – August 11
- Alma 37:11 – March 9
- Alma 37:38 – March 27
- Helaman 5:11 – June 2
- 3 Nephi 9:13 – December 23
- Ether 2:3 – July 20
- Ether 12:6 – January 12
- Mormon 9:13 – September 16

Doctrine & Covenants

- D&C 1:36 – January 29
- D&C 3:8 – April 5
- D&C 14:9 – November 26
- D&C 19:12 – August 19
- D&C 20:40 – September 15

- D&C 31:10 – February 27
- D&C 39:4 – July 5
- D&C 42:45 – December 5
- D&C 76:70 – May 9
- D&C 78:12 – September 19
- D&C 84:19 – March 14
- D&C 85:6 – March 28
- D&C 85:8 – March 3
- D&C 88:85 – December 16
- D&C 88:90 – May 8
- D&C 88:94 – October 9
- D&C 89:14 – May 6
- D&C 101:78 – January 27
- D&C 105:12 – March 31
- D&C 121:46 – July 11
- D&C 136:23 – June 16

Pearl of Great Price

- Moses 6:54 – September 7
- Moses 7:18 – April 4
- Abraham 3:26 – June 10
- J.S. Matthew 1:27 - October 22

About the Author

Phil Hudson and his wife Jan have 7 children and over 20 grandchildren. They enjoy spending time with their family at their cabin nestled in the Selkirk Mountains, on the shores of Priest Lake, the crown jewel of North Idaho. Phil had a successful family dental practice in Spokane, Washington for 43 years, before retiring in 2015. He has an eclectic mix of hobbies, and enjoys riding motorcycles and ATVs. In his free time, he can be found hiking, boating, cycling, snow biking, and traveling with Jan. He always finds time, however, to record his thoughts on his laptop. He understands Isaac Asimov's response when he was asked: "If you knew that you only had 10 minutes left to live, what would you do with your time?" He answered: "I'd type faster."

As this volume was about to be published, Phil and Jan accepted a call to serve as full time missionaries for The Church of Jesus Christ of Latter-day Saints, in the Kingdom of Tonga. While there, they will celebrate their 50th wedding anniversary.

Also by the Author

Essays

- Volume One: Spray from The Ocean of Thought
- Volume Two: Ripples on a Pond
- Volume Three: Serendipitous Meanderings
- Volume Four: Presents of Mind
- Volume Five: Mental Floss
- Volume Six: Fitness Training for the Mind and Spirit

Book of Mormon Commentary

- Born in The Wilderness
- Voices From the Dust
- Journey to Cumorah

Doctrine & Covenants Commentary

- Volume One
- Volume Two

Minute Musings: Spontaneous Combustions of Thought

- Volume One
- Volume Two
- Volume Three

Calendars:

- In His Own Words: Discovering William Tyndale
- As I Think About the Savior

Children's Books

- Muddy, Muddy
- The 13 Articles of Faith

Diode Laser Soft Tissue Surgery

- Volume One
- Volume Two
- Volume Three

These, and other titles, are available from online retailers.

www.ingramcontent.com/pod-product-compliance
Lightning Source LLC
Chambersburg PA
CBHW060505240426
43661CB00007B/919